THE PARISH CHURCHES OF ENGLAND

THE "BRITISH HERITAGE" SERIES

Uniform with this Volume

PREHISTORIC ENGLAND
By GRAHAME CLARK

THE GREATER ENGLISH
CHURCH
By HARRY BATSFORD and
CHARLES FRY

THE CATHEDRALS OF
ENGLAND
By HARRY BATSFORD and
CHARLES FRY

ENGLISH CHURCH
CRAFTSMANSHIP
By FRED H. CROSSLEY

ENGLISH CHURCH DESIGN
1040 TO 1540 A.D.
By FRED H. CROSSLEY

THE ENGLISH ABBEY
By FRED H. CROSSLEY

THE ENGLISH CASTLE
By HUGH BRAUN

THE ENGLISH COUNTRY
HOUSE
By RALPH DUTTON

THE ENGLISH GARDEN
By RALPH DUTTON

THE ENGLISH COTTAGE
By HARRY BATSFORD and
CHARLES FRY

ENGLISH VILLAGES AND
HAMLETS
By HUMPHREY PAKINGTON

ENGLISH VILLAGE HOMES
By SYDNEY R. JONES

BRITISH HILLS AND
MOUNTAINS
By BELL, BOZMAN, ETC.

THE OLD TOWNS OF
ENGLAND
By CLIVE ROUSE

THE OLD INNS OF
ENGLAND
By A. E. RICHARDSON

THE HEART OF ENGLAND
By IVOR BROWN

COUNTRYMAN'S ENGLAND
By DOROTHY HARTLEY

OLD ENGLISH
HOUSEHOLD LIFE
By GERTRUDE JEKYLL and
SYDNEY R. JONES

THE SEAS AND SHORES
OF ENGLAND
By EDMUND VALE

THE SPIRIT OF LONDON
By PAUL COHEN-PORTHEIM

THE FACE OF SCOTLAND
By HARRY BATSFORD and
CHARLES FRY

THE HEART OF SCOTLAND
By GEORGE BLAKE

THE LAND OF WALES
By EILUNED and PETER LEWIS

THE SPIRIT OF IRELAND
By LYNN DOYLE

BATSFORD BOOKS

1 CARISBROOKE CHURCH, ISLE OF WIGHT

From a Water Colour by Hugh O'Neill (1784-1824)

The British Heritage Series

THE
PARISH CHURCHES
OF ENGLAND

By

J. CHARLES COX

Edited, with Additional Chapters, by

CHARLES
BRADLEY FORD

London

B. T. BATSFORD LTD

"A church and a chapitle,
Wonderly wel y-bild,
With niches on everiche half,
And bellyche y-corven;
With crotchetes on corneres,
With knottes of gold,
With gay glitering glas
Glowyng as the sunne. . . ."

—*Crede of Piers Plowman*

First Published, March 1935
Seventh Edition, 1954

MADE AND PRINTED IN GREAT BRITAIN
TEXT BY UNWIN BROTHERS LTD., WOKING
PLATES BY THE DARIEN PRESS, EDINBURGH
FOR THE PUBLISHERS
B. T. BATSFORD LTD
4 FITZHARDINGE STREET, PORTMAN SQUARE
LONDON, W.1

CONTENTS

Page

List of Illustrations   vi

Acknowledgment   x

Chapter

ONE The Church, the Parish and the People   1

TWO The Evolution of the Parish Church: the
Arrangement and Planning   23
Types of Plan, characteristic enlargement and altera-
tion—The Clerestory—The Later Development of
the Plan—The Cross Plan—The Tower—The Porch—
The Vestry—The Crypt.

THREE The Evolution of the Parish Church: the
Structural Design *circa* 600–1820   45

FOUR Features and Fittings of Parish Churches   67
Towers, Spires and Steeples—Porches and Doorways—
Vaults and Roofs—Fittings in Stone—Fittings in
Wood—Fittings in Metal—Tombs, Monuments and
Brasses—Wall Paintings—Stained Glass.

FIVE Local Varieties in Parish Church Design   91
1. THE "SMALL STONE" TYPE.
2. THE SMALL CHURCH OF STONELESS DISTRICTS
—the Home Counties, Hampshire, Essex and Kent.
3. THE CHURCHES OF THE LIMESTONE BELT—From
Gloucestershire to Lincolnshire.
4. THE CHURCHES OF THE SOUTH-WEST—Wiltshire,
Dorset, Somerset, Devon, Cornwall.
5. THE EAST ANGLIAN TYPE OF NORFOLK AND
SUFFOLK.
6. THE CHURCHES OF THE MIDLANDS—(a) *The North
Midlands*: Leicestershire, Nottinghamshire, Derbyshire, Staffordshire; (b) *The South Midlands and
Welsh Border*: Warwickshire, Worcestershire, Monmouthshire, Herefordshire, Shropshire, Cheshire.
7. THE CHURCHES OF THE NORTH—Northumberland,
Durham, Cumberland, Westmorland, Lancashire
and Yorkshire.

Glossary of Principal Terms Used   113

Index under Counties   115

Index   121

LIST OF ILLUSTRATIONS

Figure   *Page*
1   Carisbrooke Church, Isle of Wight   *Frontispiece*
2   Alabaster Panel of the Resurrection   *Facing* x
3   Wrington, Somerset: The Church and Tower   1
4   St. Botolph's Church, Boston, Lincolnshire   2
5   Fingest, Buckinghamshire   *Between* 2 and 3
6   Penn, Buckinghamshire   2 and 3
7   Oundle, Northamptonshire   *Facing* 3
8   Whitbourne, Herefordshire   4
9   Louth, Lincolnshire: The Tower and Spire   5
10   Long Melford, Suffolk: A fifteenth-century "Wool"
        Church   8
11   Fairford, Gloucestershire   9
12   St. Petrock's Church, Bodmin, Cornwall   9
13   Gresham, Norfolk: Relief Panel on the Font   12
14   Bench-end Carving in Tideswell Church, Derby-
        shire   12
15 and 16   Culbone, Somerset   13
17   Walpole St. Peter, Norfolk   16
18   Mullion, Cornwall   17
19   St. Thomas of Canterbury, Salisbury   17
20   Jacobean Fittings in Croscombe Church, Somerset   20
21   An English Renaissance Interior, Avington, Hamp-
        shire   21
22   Wedmore, Somerset   22
23   Whitby, Yorkshire: A Georgian Interior   22
24   Witney, Oxfordshire   23
25   Brixworth, Northamptonshire   24
26   The Saxon Chapel, Bradford-on-Avon, Wiltshire   24
27   The Heath Chapel, Shropshire   25
28   Stewkley, Buckinghamshire: The Nave and Tower   28
29   Walpole St. Peter, Norfolk   28
30   St. John's Church, Devizes, Wiltshire   29
31   Ipplepen Church, Devonshire   30
32   Flint-built thatched Church at Hales, Norfolk   31
33   Uffington Church, Berkshire   31
34   Tilney All Saints, Norfolk   32
35   Lavenham, Suffolk   33
36   Stratford-on-Avon, Warwickshire: The Chancel   33
37   Terrington St. Clement, Norfolk   34

vi

Figure		Page
38	St. Cuthbert's, Wells, Somerset	*Between* 34 and 35
39	Saffron Walden, Essex	34 and 35
40	St. Mary's, Bury St. Edmunds, Suffolk	*Facing* 35
41	Long Sutton, Lincolnshire	36
42	The Norman Church at Old Shoreham, Sussex	37
43	Breamore, Hampshire	37
44	A fine Cruciform Church, Doulting, Somerset	38
45	Patrington Church, Yorkshire, from the east	39
46	The detached Bell-tower, West Walton, Norfolk	42
47	Cirencester, Gloucestershire	43
48	The Hamlet Church at Great Bookham, Surrey	44
49	The Interior of St. Cuthbert's, Wells, Somerset	45
50	Escomb, County Durham: The Saxon Chancel	48
51	Bessingham, Norfolk	48
52	Greenstead-juxta-Ongar, Essex	49
53	St. Peter's, Northampton	49
54	Elkstone, Gloucestershire	50
55	Norman Grotesques at Kilpeck, Herefordshire	50
56	The Norman Nave, Melbourne, Derbyshire	51
57	Castle Hedingham, Essex: The Nave Arcade	51
58	Stone, Kent: The thirteenth-century Interior	52
59	West Walton, Norfolk	53
60	Thaxted, Essex	53
61	Great Brington, Northamptonshire: The Arcade	56
62	Gothic Capitals: West Country Perpendicular	57
63	Gothic Capitals: Decorated	57
64	Gothic Capitals: Early English	57
65	Patrington, Yorkshire	58
66, 67	Gothic Window Tracery: Geometrical	59
68	Gothic Window Tracery: Curvilinear	59
69	Gothic Window Tracery: Early Perpendicular	59
70	The Greenway Chapel, Tiverton, Devon	60
71	Curry Rivel Church, Somerset	60
72	Lavenham Church, Suffolk	61
73	The Arcade, Deeping St. James, Lincolnshire	62
74	The Nave, Long Melford, Suffolk	62
75	Norwich: St. Peter Mancroft Church	*Between* 62 and 63
76	Ashburton, Devon	62 and 63
77	St. Stephen's, Walbrook, London	*Facing* 63
78	Renaissance Church Exteriors: Blandford, Dorset	64
79	Renaissance Church Exteriors: Glynde, Sussex	64

Figure		Page
80	Renaissance Church Interiors: Tyberton, Herefordshire	Facing 65
81	Renaissance Church Interiors: St. Paul's Walden, Hertfordshire	65
82	Earls Barton, Northamptonshire	68
83	Olney, Buckinghamshire	Between 68 and 69
84	St. Leonard's, Shoreditch, London	Between 68 and 69
85	Spires of the Stone Belt: Ketton, Rutland	Facing 69
86	Spires of the Stone Belt: Higham Ferrers, Northamptonshire	69
87	Fifteenth-century Porches: Crowcombe, Somerset	72
88	Fifteenth-century Porches: St. Nicholas', King's Lynn, Norfolk	72
89	East Dereham, Norfolk: The Font	73
90	Aconbury, Herefordshire: The Timber West Porch	73
91	March, Cambridgeshire	76
92	Higher Bickington, Devon: Carved Bench-ends	76
93	Fifteenth-century Timber Roofs: Necton, Norfolk	77
94	Fifteenth-century Timber Roofs: Dean, Bedfordshire	77
95	The Easter Sepulchre, Hawton, Nottinghamshire	80
96	The Sprying Family Pew, Lavenham, Suffolk	80
97	The Sculptured Reredos, Bampton, Oxfordshire	81
98	Misericord at Ludlow, Shropshire	81
99	An Alabaster Relief, Long Melford, Suffolk	81
100	Late medieval Font-cover, Ufford, Suffolk	82
101	Late medieval Font-cover, Halifax, Yorkshire	82
102	Wiggenhall, St. Mary-the-Virgin, Norfolk	Between 82 and 83
103	Carved Stallwork, Nantwich, Cheshire	82 and 83
104	Screen and Pulpit, South Burlingham, Norfolk	82 and 83
105	St. Woolos, Newport, Monmouthshire	82 and 83
106	Plymtree, Devon	Facing 83
107	The Screen and Rood-Loft, Dennington, Suffolk	84
108	Carved Screen Detail, Bovey Tracey, Devon	85
109	Wrought Ironwork, Eaton Bray, Bedfordshire	85
110	Framlingham, Suffolk	86
111	Alabaster Effigies, Lowick, Northamptonshire	87
112	A Squint, Blewbury, Berkshire	87
113	A late medieval tomb, St. Mark's Chapel, Bristol	90
114	Elmley Castle, Worcestershire	90
115	St. Thomas of Canterbury, Salisbury	Between 90 and 91
116	Wall-painting, Breage, Cornwall	90 and 91

viii

Figure		Page
117	Screen Paintings, Somerleyton, Suffolk *Between* 90 and 91	
118	Screen Paintings, Wolborough, Devon	90 and 91
119	Chesham, Buckinghamshire	*Facing* 91
120	Lelant Church, Cornwall	94
121	Heckington Church, Lincolnshire	94
122	Litlington, Sussex	*Between* 94 and 95
123	Harescombe, Gloucestershire	94 and 95
124	Merstham Church, Surrey	94 and 95
125	Knebworth Church, Hertfordshire	94 and 95
126	Blackmore, Essex	*Facing* 95
127	Sandon, Essex	95
128	The detached Belfry, Pembridge, Herefordshire	96
129	New Romney, Kent	96
130	East Harling, Norfolk	97
131	Boughton Aluph Church, Kent	97
132	Chipping Campden, Gloucestershire	100
133	Thornbury Tower, Gloucestershire	100
134	Warboys, Huntingdonshire	101
135	Broach Spires: Pickworth, Lincolnshire	102
136	Broach Spires: Upper Hambleton, Rutland	102
137	Woodford Church, Northamptonshire	
		Between 102 and 103
138	Puddletown, Dorset	102 and 103
139	West Alvington, Devon	102 and 103
140	Launceston, Cornwall	102 and 103
141	Huish Episcopi, Somerset	*Facing* 103
142	St. Neots Church, Cornwall	104
143	Acle, Norfolk	105
144	The fifteenth-century Tower, Eye, Suffolk	108
145	Rockfield Church, Monmouthshire	109
146	Timbered Towers: Pirton, Worcestershire	110
147	Timbered Towers: Warndon, Worcestershire	110
148	Heysham, Lancashire	111
149	Skipwith, Yorkshire	111

ACKNOWLEDGMENT

THE publishers wish to acknowledge their obligation to the photographers whose work is reproduced in these pages, namely, the late Dr. Granville Buckley, for Fig. 66 (from the collection of the Courtauld Institute of Art, University of London); Mr. J. Allan Cash, F.R.P.S., for Fig. 4; Central Press Photos, for Fig. 125; the late B. C. Clayton, for Figs. 25, 28, 32, 50, 53, 55, 57, 73, 74, 80, 86, 90, 93, 98, 99, 102, 103, 105, 106, 109, 114, 123, 126, 127, 132, 133, 135, 136; Mr. F. H. Crossley, for Figs. 45, 62, 63, 64, 68, 69, 101, 108, 110, 111; Mr. J. Dixon-Scott, for Figs. 20, 54, 88, 112, 138; Messrs. Dolby Bros., for Fig. 85; Mr. Herbert Felton, F.R.P.S., for Figs. 8, 42, 51, 75, 128, 131, 143, 146, 147, 148; Mr. W. H. A. Fincham, for Fig. 96; Messrs. Fox Photos, Ltd., for Fig. 47; Messrs. F. Frith & Co., Ltd., for Figs. 15, 23, 39, 49, 60, 120, 139, 140, 145; Messrs. Gibson & Son, of Penzance, for Fig. 116; Mr. F. A. Girling, for Fig. 144; Mr. P. Goodchild, for Figs. 17, 59; Mr. A. W. Haggis, for Figs. 13, 71, 89, 115, 117, 118; Mr. A. H. Hawke, for Fig. 18; the late F. E. Howard, for Figs. 100, 107; Mr. A. F. Kersting, F.R.P.S., for Figs. 26, 121; Messrs. Keystone View Co., for Fig. 79; Messrs. Photochrom Co., Ltd., for Fig. 137; Mr. T. E. Routh, for Fig. 56; Mr. H. J. Smith, for Figs. 43, 94; The Rev. F. Sumner and the Rev. F. R. P. Sumner, for Figs. 16, 19, 22, 31, 38, 70, 92, 95, 97, 104, 113, 130; Mr. H. Irving Taylor, for Figs. 35, 67, 91, 124; Mr. Will F. Taylor, for Figs. 3, 4, 5, 6, 7, 9, 10, 11, 12, 21, 24, 27, 30, 33, 34, 36, 37, 40, 41, 44, 46, 48, 58, 61, 65, 72, 76, 77, 82, 83, 84, 119, 122, 129, 134, 141, 142; Mr. H. Walker, for Fig. 14; Mr. Reece Winstone, A.R.P.S., for Fig. 78.

Thanks are also due to the Keeper of the Wallace Collection for permission to reproduce Fig. 2; to Mr. W. Curtis Green, R.A., for the fine drawings on pages 22 and 90, and to Miss M. Weinstock for her draft of the County Index, which has been adapted and incorporated, with additions to the general index.

2 ALABASTER PANEL OF THE RESURRECTION: English, Fifteenth Century

3 WRINGTON, SOMERSET: The Fifteenth-century Church and Tower

CHAPTER ONE

The Church, the Parish and the People

COLLECTIVELY, the parish churches form England's most characteristic contribution to Gothic art. While, by the fine work of the National Trust and other bodies, early secular buildings of every kind are increasingly given the status of public monuments, these fabrics remain the active centres of life that they have been, in certain cases, for a thousand years or more. Some of them are rich with the gifts of English craftsmanship; others have come into being unobtrusively in answer to the needs of remote and backward country communities. Very few have come down to us intact in their original forms; those that have not known sudden change have responded to a long process of structural evolution that has hardly finished at the present day, and all owe their preservation in some degree to the generations of parishioners that have guarded them against the slow decay of time and the weather.

Individually, they represent such a range of types, sizes, materials, plans and grouping that to produce a systematic account of them in a short space is almost impossible. From the large town fabric to the small hamlet church, it is safe to assert that no two could be found closely alike; each has its architectural "personality," and each combines with its surroundings to produce its familiar local "picture." The well-recognised strains of individualism and conservatism in the English character are strongly represented in the growth of these churches—the former in the vigour and versatility of their design, the latter in their frequent retention of old work side by side with the new. Though a thoroughgoing reconstruction could be undertaken without scruple, there was generally in this country a feeling for the intentions of earlier builders that found expression in an adherence to old dimensions, and even in an occasional re-incorporation of old features.

Historically, these churches have played such an important part in the life of England for nine centuries that it will be well to preface an account of their evolution with a summary, however slight, of the tremendous chapter in social development that they represent. As nine out of ten of those under

I

review are of medieval origin, this chapter will concern itself chiefly with parish life and organisation between the Norman Conquest of 1066 and the Reformation of *circa* 1535—a vast subject, which it may seem impertinent to attempt to condense into a few pages. Nevertheless, it is one essential to the understanding and appreciation of the buildings, and a rapid sketch may at least serve to record the outlines of its wide, varied and often shadowy perspective.

The parish itself may be defined as the community of a fixed area, organised for Church purposes and recognising as its communal and spiritual centre the church fabric. Its elements are thus threefold: the building, the people and the priest's office of the cure of souls. The first partitioning of the country into such areas is a subject of much obscurity, but it is probable that in the beginning the manor or township was usually the determining unit. Their extent, of course, varied enormously— as it varies to-day—from matters of acres to matters of square miles. In a remote district a parish might embrace a whole chain of manors; where habitation was thicker, it might equally well follow the boundaries of a single demesne. When map-making was still a rare accomplishment, the extent of a parish would often be confirmed annually by a "beating of the bounds," still occasionally practised as a survival.[1]

The parochial system was inaugurated in Saxon times, and brought to maturity following the Councils of London and Westminster during the twelfth century. Its financial basis was a system of "tithes," or offerings to the Church of a tenth part of the produce of the parish lands, whether in money or in kind. This system, as will appear later in the chapter, grew open to grave abuses, and it was seldom latterly that a priest had the administration of the parish funds, of which, by an early teaching of the Church, a fourth part should have been offered to the Bishop if he required it, a fourth to the priest for his living, a fourth to the poor, and a fourth devoted to the maintenance of the fabric. Later, it became an accepted tradition that the rector, or administrator of the tithes, should maintain the chancel only from these funds, the parishioners holding themselves responsible for the rest.

The earliest parish priests, if they may be called such, were the chaplains of the Saxon Thanes, who themselves often took deacons' orders to inherit the benefices and tithes of their parishes. The chaplains probably ranked merely as upper servants; and it was due to an enduring pre-Conquest tradition that the advowson, or presentation-right of a benefice,

[1] Miss C. Hole, *English Custom and Usage*, 1941.

4 BOSTON, LINCOLNSHIRE: St. Botolph's Church and "Stump"
from the South

7   OUNDLE, NORTHAMPTONSHIRE : Detail of South Transept,
South Porch and Tower

has continued to remain with the lord of the manor throughout the Middle Ages and in many cases down to the present
day. At the same time, in all matters pertaining to the parish,
the rector was bound by the episcopal authority, and could be
removed from his living only by a complicated process of
canonical law and for a grave offence.

The actual initiation of most church buildings remains
conjectural, though it may be assumed that the majority, in
Saxon and early Norman times at least, owed their origin to
a local Thane or Lord, serving primarily as chapels for himself, his household and his dependants. Of the thousands of
country churches covered by the scope of this book, the
greater part are of early, or definitely pre-Conquest, foundation.
It is an exciting thought that many of their sites have been
in the same use for an unbroken thousand years, and that some
possibly mark the meeting and burial places of earlier religions
and races. It must have been more than a coincidence that the
first churches were constantly built in the proximity of prehistoric mounds.

Though in certain cases the incentives to early building are to
be traced, while later construction had often manifestly for its
impulse the pride and vigour of growing communities, there
is still much to be discovered of the circumstances under
which church fabrics came into being during the Middle
Ages—who commissioned them and who bore the expense.
The idea that the monasteries provided sums for the construction or reconstruction of churches in any large numbers
is, of course, discredited; nevertheless, their existence poses
a problem that continues to be neglected by scholars, rather
strangely in view of its importance and bearing on social
history. So conscientious an inquirer as Edmund Sharpe stood
mystified before the "new star" outburst of Curvilinear
grandeur in one small area of Lincolnshire, apparently regard-
ing as inadequate the tentative suggestion then current of a
single local benefactor on a grand scale.

It is certain, of course, that throughout the medieval
period a proportion of churches at least continued to be
founded, rebuilt or enlarged at the expense of individual
patrons, whether royalty, nobles or ecclesiastics possessed of
many manors, or local gentlemen living on their own lands. An
early pretext was as a thank-offering for a safe return from
a Crusade; but even after the development of a proper
diocesan organisation during the twelfth century, a resident lord would generally find his local pride involved
in matters of maintenance and improvement. Early in the

fourteenth century we find Sir William Trussell, lord of the manor of Shottesbrooke in Berkshire, entirely reconstructing the parish church, with a college for a warden and five priests; and as late as the sixteenth century a Cornish squire, Sir Henry Trecarrel, bore the considerable cost of rebuilding the great granite church of St. Mary Magdalene at Launceston (*circa* 1520) (140), with its singular profusion of external carving. A local "Lady Bountiful," then as now, would be a frequent donor; she can be seen in medieval miniatures, in her tall white headdress, inspecting the work in progress. A case in point was Dame Katerine of Burgh, who in 1412 entered into contract with one Richard of Cracall, mason, "to make the Kirke of Ketericke [Catterick] newe als werkmanschippe and mason crafte will." At Lavenham in Suffolk, the cost of the great new church (35) building between 1480 and 1530 was borne jointly by John De Vere, Earl of Oxford, the lord of the manor, and the Spryngs, a famous local family of clothiers, enriched in the wool boom that had made the fortune of the district—an interesting combination of the old order and the new.

Sometimes an ecclesiastic bore the cost, as Bishop Robert Burnell of Bath and Wells, who *circa* 1200 rebuilt the pleasant little church still standing at his native Acton Burnell in Shropshire; and the splendid fabric of Heckington in Lincolnshire (121) was reconstructed during the fourteenth century almost undoubtedly at the charge of a wealthy rector. In 1408–15, the chancel of Adderbury Church in Oxfordshire was rebuilt at the expense of the lord of the manor—in this case New College, Oxford, which, under the bequest of its founder, William of Wykeham, held the administration of the tithes. Royal patronage produced the nave and tower, added by the Duke of York in 1434 to an older collegiate chancel, at Fotheringay in Northamptonshire, and, as a special instance, the church of Battlefield near Shrewsbury, raised by command of Henry IV on the site of the victory that established his crown.

Particularly during the later Middle Ages, when town life became a growing factor in social development, we find the parishioners as a body initiating quite substantial building schemes. While the maintenance of the nave had always been their responsibility, the number of cases increased in which the entire cost of reconstruction was borne by the parish, as in *circa* 1400 at Broadhempston in Devon, when a petition was laid before the Bishop of Exeter for permission to rebuild the parish church of St. Petrock, which was ruinous, on a larger scale and in another part of the churchyard. This was

8 WHITBOURNE, HEREFORDSHIRE: The Fourteenth-century
Tower and Lych-gate

9 LOUTH, **LINCOLNSHIRE**: The Fifteenth-century Tower and Spire

allowed conditional on the work being completed within two years, and a special indulgence was granted to all who contributed to the cost. While indulgences were probably a frequent incentive to money-raising, it would be churlish to discount the real enthusiasm and generosity of communities such as the townsmen of Bodmin, who in 1469–71 expended the sum of £268 17s. 9½d.—the equivalent of some £5,000 in modern money—on the rebuilding of their church (12), in addition to gifts of materials in kind. "Many who gave money gave labour also" (we quote from Vol. VII of the *Camden Miscellany* for 1875), "many who could not give money laboured as best they might, and others gave what they could. We have gifts of lambs, of a cow, and of a goose; and one woman, in addition to her subscription, sold her 'crokke' [metal cauldron] for 20d.; and all found its way into the common treasury. . . . We find a 'hold woman' contributing 3s. 2½d.; while the maidens in Fore Street and Bore Street gave subscriptions, in addition to the sums received from the Gilds of Virgins in the same streets. The Vicar gave his year's salary, and the 'parish pepell' who lived outside the town contributed 19s. . . ."

At Bodmin there were some forty religious gilds at this time, which probably embraced the majority of the townspeople. Beyond the funds they raised, these organisations would have played a large part in stimulating local enthusiasm; and of course, as they flourished, the gilds often grew to be quite ambitious builders on their own account. Their character was fraternal and charitable, and each was dedicated to the cult of a patron saint. An important object was the provision of regular masses for the souls of dead members, so that a large gild would often require its own chapel, preferably in the parish church, and its own chaplain—particularly in important towns such as Coventry (*vide* p. 37). Gilds were founded by individuals, by groups of friends, or by trades; thus, in 1338, Geoffrey Wynchecombe and another built a chapel in honour of St. Katherine on the south side of the vanished St. Mary Colechurch, London, and founded a fraternity to provide lights and a chaplain. In this case, the modest size of the building made a structural addition essential; and it will be seen in the next chapter how frequently an increase in gild membership resulted in the enlargement of a chapel or the reconstruction of an aisle. Sometimes even the rebuilding of an entire church was undertaken by a gild, as was the case at St. Magnus, London Bridge, in the second half of the fourteenth century.

Additions to parish churches also frequently resulted from bequests. This was the case with the north aisle of St. Mary's at Beverley, for the building of which Robert Dacres, a weaver of the town, left £16. Generally the testator would provide for the foundation of a chantry, or office for the saying of masses for his soul over a period of years or "in perpetuity," for which, if the endowment sufficed, a permanent chapel and chaplain might be necessary. In parish churches, chantry chapels of this kind became innumerable, and were as a rule built adjoining the chancel (though in many other positions as well), often forming the nuclei of later aisles. Sometimes an entire aisle would be of chantry foundation, as was the case at Hornby in Lancashire, where it was endowed by two priests. At Lavenham, the north and south chancel chapels were both chantries, added on the completion of the church (*circa* 1530), the former by Simon Branch and his wife Elizabeth, the latter by Thomas Spryng the younger, whose inscription appears below the external battlements. At Wingfield in Suffolk there is an extreme case. Here the endowment of Sir John Wingfield was so ambitious that, under the terms of his will, the church was pulled down and rebuilt *circa* 1362 as a quire of chantry priests, ruled over by a warden, of whom the second in seniority was reckoned the sacristan and had the cure of souls. The college building nearby survives as a farm.

It will be seen, then, that the contributions of the faithful, direct or indirect, were varied, embracing almost every walk of life. That they were frequent appears from the introduction of such a measure as the Statute of Mortmain of 1279, which sought to divert at least a part of this steady stream of funds from the Church exchequer. Apart from spiritual aspects of the case, the pride and pleasure of medieval people in their churches was very real, and the local patriotism that, in the bad state of communications, enhanced the rivalries between town and town, parish and parish, often found its proudest expression in the church building. With the exception of the castles, which always absorbed a percentage of the labour, the majority of the funds and skill available was concentrated on the raising of churches. The status and organisation of the groups of men who brought these buildings into being is perhaps worth examining briefly before passing on to deal with matters of parish administration.

Quite early in the Middle Ages, the various trades connected with building had become organised, each controlled by its shadowy but autocratic "Mistery and Gild," in which a workman graduated by apprenticeship. There were gilds of masons, carpenters, plumbers, glaziers, plasterers, tilers, smiths ("black" and "white"), and so on, most of whom would participate in the building of a church. The senior craft was generally that of the mason, and the master-mason supervising the work as a whole was thus the nearest medieval approximation to the modern architect.

The scattered nature of the work sometimes made the mason's life a nomadic one; he would wander from place to place, working here a couple of months and there a couple o years, eager to hear of employment and joining in the general cross-country trek when the chance of it arose—Dr. Coulton has very charmingly reconstructed this nomadism in his own part of Norfolk in his "Wander Years."[1] A result was the speedy propagation of the newest mason-fashions even in remote places—though here it must be remembered that there were also times, particularly in the period of depletion that followed the Black Death, when a scarcity of masons set their services at a premium, and empressment was regularly resorted to for the Royal Works, rather after the fashion of the naval press-gang of the eighteenth century.

As soon as it was decided to embark on building work, the masters in the various trades would be chosen, who in their turn enrolled subordinates of the several recognised grades. These latter varied widely at different periods. The free- (or freestone) mason was, of course, always a skilled craftsman, and ranged from the ordinary stone-dresser responsible for the plain fabric of any building to the specialised sculptor of delicate figuring and ornament. The heavier work was generally undertaken by "rough masons," "hewers," and "layers," often with subordinate labourers outside the craft for such tasks as mortaring and carrying. A "lodge" would be established adjoining the work in progress—a temporary structure of canvas or timber and thatch, generally heated in the winter—which was the workshop, club-room and sometimes dwelling of the craftsmen employed. This would be built by the carpenters, who also in many cases provided carts, tackle, scaffoldings and timber-centerings for the masonry. The master worked with the others at the bench, undertaking some of the more difficult tasks and supervising the setting-out and organisation. An average master's wage during the fifteenth century ranged from 8d. to 12d. a day, occasionally with the yearly gift of a gown or other perquisites in kind, and a freemason received from 4d. to 6d.

The organisation also varied with the scale of the job and

---

[1] *Art and the Reformation*, 1928.

C

the requirements of the patron at different periods. The allocation of the subordinate work was particularly inconsistent, even the freemason from time to time being called upon to quarry the stone that he later dressed, as was the case at Bodmin. A good illustration of procedure during the early fifteenth century is the case of Adderbury, already referred to, where the chancel was rebuilt between 1408 and 1418 at the expense of New College; for here a record of the accounts and payments is still in existence. The master-mason in general charge was Richard Winchcombe, who afterwards supervised the building of the Oxford Divinity School; John Berewyk, who kept a day-book and tallies, seems to have been little more than a paymaster and accountant, under the strict supervision of the college officials. Winchcombe worked personally on the tracery of the great east window, where he was assisted by an apprentice—a common practice of the Middle Ages, exactly analogous to the modern artisan and his mate. This combination was paid at several rates, ranging from 4s. 10d. to 6s. 1d. a week. The standard rates for masons varied from 2s. 6d. to 3s. a week in the summer to 1s. 8d. to 2s. 6d. a week for the three darkest months of winter. Fifteen masons were employed in all, but never more than nine at the same time.

Both here and at Bodmin a certain amount of "contract" work figures in the rolls; in other words, a master would periodically engage himself to carry out specific jobs for a lump sum, inclusive of labour and sometimes also of materials and cartage. This system hardly makes its appearance until after the Black Death, and was then seldom of universal application. At the same time, it enabled an astute member of a trade to rise from the position of a weekly wage-earner to that of an independent capitalist on a small scale, sometimes even possessed of his own quarries, as was the case with the famous Westminster mason, Henry Yevele, towards the close of the fourteenth century—possibly the first English architect. Several contracts for parish-church building are on record, one of the most interesting being that for the nave and tower of Fotheringay, dated 1434 and made between the representatives of the Duke of York and William Horwood, freemason, "to make up a new body of a kirk joyning to the quire of the college of Fodringhey of the same hight and brede that the said quire is of. . . . And in this cuvenant the said Will. Horwood shal also wel make all the groundwerk [i.e. foundations] of the said body. . . . And . . . shal make two isles . . . according to hight and brede of the isles of the saide quire, and in hight to the body aforesaid . . . and alle the

10 LONG MELFORD, SUFFOLK: A stately "Wool" Church of the Fifteenth Century in East Anglian Flint. The Tower is modern

11 FAIRFORD, GLOUCESTERSHIRE: Another Fifteenth-century
"Wool" Church, famous for its Glass

12 BODMIN, CORNWALL: The Church of St. Petrock, rebuilt by
the Townsmen in the early Fifteenth Century

remanent of the saide body and isles unto the full hight of the said quire with clene hewen ashler altogedir in the outer side unto the full hight of the said quire; and all the inner side of rough-stone, except the bench-table-stones, the soles of the windows, the pillars and chapetrels that the arches and pendants shall rest upon, which shall be altogedir of free-stone wrought trewly and dewly as hit ought to be."

The specification goes on to include "wyndows of free-stone, accordying in all poynts unto the wyndows of the said quire," and four-light windows at the ends of the aisles. Each aisle was to have "six mighty botrasse of free-stone, clen-hewyn; and every botrasse fynisht with a fynial." There was to be a "cler-story both withyn & without . . . made of clene asheler growndid upon ten mighty pillars, with four respounds." At the west end was to be a "stepyll standing [above] the chirche upon three strong and mighty arches vawthid with stoon." In this case, "my said lord of Yorke shall fynde the carriage and stuffe; that is to say stone, lyme, sonde, ropes, boltes, ladderis, tymbre, scaffolds, gynnes, and all manere of stuffe that belongeth to the said werk, for which werk, well, truly and duly to be made and fiynisht . . . the said Will. Horwoode shall haf of my said lord CCC I Sterlingues"— which was to be paid in regular instalments by measure as the building grew in height. In the case of Horwood's failure to complete the work to schedule, he bound himself uncompromisingly to "yeilde his body to prison at my lordys wyll, and all his movable goods and heritages at my said lordys disposition and ordenance."

Though it is only possible to treat this great subject very cursorily, these notes and extracts may at least serve to provide the reader with a rough idea of the circumstances under which parish churches were normally built and enlarged during the Middle Ages. It remains now to show something of how they were attended and served, and the type of men who served them. Among the thousands of ecclesiastics that thronged Catholic England in increasing numbers as the Middle Ages advanced, three grades must be considered particularly in connection with the parish churches. The first is the resident and working rector, who represented the parochial system as it was intended to be, and does not figure very largely in the records. Appointed by the lord of the manor, he was, as has been seen, solely answerable to the bishop in parochial matters, and had the administration of the tithes. As the religious orders began to flourish in the twelfth century, however, it became almost a fashion for holders of advowsons to bequeath or transfer these to monasteries, which, by a variety of means, generally also obtained from the bishop the rectorial status and tithes. The monastery would then appoint a deputy or "vicar" in secular orders to serve the parish as its nominee, granting him for his living either a fixed stipend or a minor portion of the tithes, the majority of which, of course, went to increase its own revenues. This arrangement, though sometimes satisfactory in practice, was open to all the abuses of a "farming" system. To counteract the growing conception of the vicar as a mere servant of the monastery, dismissable at will, the Church insisted, at the Council of Westminster presided over by Anselm in 1102, that his appointment should be a permanent one, subject to the institution and discipline of the bishop, thus bringing into being a new status of clergy, the "perpetual vicars."

In other cases, prelates and influential men in orders, including occasionally foreign papal nominees, and such religious bodies as a dean and chapter, came to hold whole chains of rectories, which, though bringing them in a considerable income, they seldom if ever visited, leaving the cure of souls to salaried vicars of their own appointment. Thus in 1362 we find the Bishop of Norwich, in granting a licence for the foundation of the chantry college at Wingfield in Suffolk, complaining that "not a few rectors of parish Churches in our Diocese, being secular clerks (some of them being occupied with the business of their lords, others engaged in completing their studies), frequently commit the cure of their parish Churches to hired chaplains whom they pay, and who are rather day-labourers than pastors." This pluralism, which had its later parallel in eighteenth-century England, was one of the worst evils of the medieval Church, though it seems to have been accepted complacently and almost as a matter of course by some of the most enlightened figures of the age, including men of the stature of St. Thomas Cantilupe of Hereford.

The third grade in question was the chantry priest, whose office has already been touched upon. While, when attached to a parish church altar, he must always to some extent have helped the priest with his duties, besides possible teaching in school, he must not be confused with the salaried curate or chaplain who was occasionally necessary as an assistant. Beyond his daily quota of duty masses, his office, where the endowment was slight, was probably as meagre as its emoluments, and it does not seem unnatural that there was often difficulty in finding priests at all to serve chantries of the leaner sort. Of course, where funds were plentiful, it was a different matter, and the duties of a chantry priest were then obviously more congenial to the leisurely minded than the cure of souls.

The workaday parish priest, it may be assumed, was often regarded a little contemptuously by the other orders; and it is certain that his origin was frequently a quite humble one, as is the case in Ireland and Italy to the present day. Chaucer's parson had a ploughman for his brother, and Langland rails angrily at the peasant manners and origin of some of the clergy of his age. That this was the case is not surprising, since the emoluments of "perpetual vicars" were often deplorably meagre. Cases of ignorance and ill-living could, of course, be quoted pretty extensively, particularly during the fifteenth century, when the standard of the priesthood was at its lowest; there are records of parsons who could neither construe nor sing the Mass, and Myrk's fatherly *Instructions to Parish Priests*, a famous rhyming manual of the Middle Ages, stated explicitly that bad Latin would not prejudice the efficacy of a baptism; all a priest had to do was to enunciate the first syllable of each word correctly, and the child would be well and truly christened. Langland's "Sloth" in *Piers Plowman*, the first of a long series of English sporting parsons, could "find a hare in a field or in a furrow better than construe the first Psalm or explain it to the parish."

The system of episcopal or archidiaconal "visitations," which seems to have been fairly regularly maintained, required the appointment by the parish of "sidesmen" (or *synods-men*) who would report confidentially to the authorities on each incumbent. It may be remarked that such visitations were often a heavy financial burden on a parish, and if the bishop took it into his head to come in person, it might spell disaster to an entire community. The four following entries, taken almost at random from the register of Bishop Stapledon of Exeter for the year 1301, give interesting sidelights on the character of the average country parson at this time :—

CLYST HONITON.—They say that their parish priest is of honest life and good conversation, and hath been there 22 years, honestly fulfilling his priestly office in all that pertaineth to a parish priest; but he is now broken with age and insufficient for the cure of the parish.

DAWLISH.—They say that the Vicar, whom they hold for a good man, resideth not personally, but hath in his place sir Adam, a Chaplain, who beareth himself well and honestly and teacheth them excellently in spiritual things. But Randolph the Chaplain hath kept his concubine for ten years or more; and though often rebuked, he persisteth incorrigibly. The parish clerk is continent and honest.

ST. MARY CHURCH.—The parishioners say that, until the days of the present Vicar, they were wont to maintain the Chancel in all things and to be immune from paying tithe for the restoration of the Church; but the present Vicar, though he maintaineth not the Chancel, yet receiveth the tithe and compelleth them to pay. . . .

STAVERTON.—They say that Sir Walter, the Vicar, beareth himself well and honestly, and teacheth them excellently in spiritual things; nor is there, as they assert, any defect in him. Of hidden mortal sin they know naught. And his Vicarage, as they assert, is worth ten marks.

These extracts well support the assumption that, working side by side with the ignorant and the illiterate, often under anything but ideal conditions, were always to be found parish priests as simple and exemplary in their lives and duties as Chaucer's "poor parson of the town" in *The Canterbury Tales*. In their humble cottage-rectories, these men would dispense such comfort and counsel to their peasant flocks as were theirs to give, and satisfy as funds allowed the priestly obligations of offering shelter to strangers and alms to the sick and destitute. In addition to their stipends or tithes, there were always, of course, the oblations of the faithful—free-will offerings in money or in kind; and while their general mode of living was possibly little in advance of that of their parishioners, the glebe farmlands would at least furnish them with a sufficiency of larder produce for their daily needs.

During the later Middle Ages, the parishioners were represented in church matters by their elected wardens, much as they are to-day. The first appearance of these as early as the thirteenth century was possibly a result of the abuses of tithe appropriation, owing to which, in an increasing number of cases, the responsibility for the upkeep of the fabric tended to devolve, as at St. Mary Church, on the parishioners. Gifts and bequests to the parish were often abundant, in country districts generally in kind, varying from a tract of farmland to a pound of wax for the Paschal Candle, or the favourite present of the humble, a rosary. There are instances of quite large estates accruing to parishes, and of side altars being maintained from the profits of individual flocks of sheep. The churchwardens acted as trustees for the people in the administration of these revenues, and supervised the provision of furniture, vestments, hangings, bells, candles, and other things needed to maintain the beauty and dignity of the services. In most parishes, people's collections were taken at regular intervals, and money-making festivities were promoted, such as the traditional "hock-tyde," still observed in some Berkshire parishes, with

13 THE MASS : Relief Panel on the Font at Gresham, Norfolk

14 A BAPTISM : Bench-end Carving in Tideswell Church, Derbyshire

15, 16 CULBONE, SOMERSET: The Smallest Complete Church in England
in its Exmoor Combe—inside and out

its mimed capture of the womenfolk in the churchyard and their release in return for a donation, and the popular parish "ales," that continued into the eighteenth century and after. As early as the fifteenth century there are cases on record of a parish rate being levied by the wardens on their own assessment. Another duty was the handing over of moral delinquents for judgment to the archdeacon's court.

Other parish officials were the clerk or holy-water bearer, the sexton, the bellman, and occasionally the schoolmaster. The first, while originally often a candidate for orders, was latterly seldom more than a salaried verger, serving the priest at Mass and responsible for the decent appearance of the church. An important duty was the house-to-house sprinkling around the parish of the holy water consecrated by the priest each Sunday, for which he would receive regular gifts from the householders. The sexton's office remains to the present day, but the bellman's has largely disappeared, for, besides supervising the ringings for services and funerals (the latter a regular source of revenue), he was also used as a kind of parish crier, proclaiming with a hand-bell in every street the particular *obits* and masses of the morrow, to remind gild-members of their obligations, as at St. Botolph's at Boston: "For the sowles of Richard Chapeman & Alys his wyf, brother and syster of Corpus Christi Gylde, to-morne shall be theyre yere-day."

The frequency of daily masses varied with the parish. In great town churches they would be almost unceasing, but in country districts the usual arrangement was an early "Morrow Mass" for travellers at about 6 a.m., probably at a side altar of chantry foundation, followed by High Mass at eight or nine, at which a good number of the villagers would be present. England was famous for its devotion to the daily service; after it, however, the church would probably stay silent for the rest of the day, save for an occasional *Salve* to the Virgin in the early evening. Sundays generally began with an early Mattins, followed by the consecration of holy water before the Rood, and often a procession of the clergy and congregation, censing and sprinkling water in each part of the building, and, in the country, sometimes making the complete outside circuit of the church. High Mass followed, and Vespers between two and three in the afternoon completed the Sunday round of observance.

While formal and more or less stereotyped sermons were probably introduced into the Mass—following the reading of the Gospel—from quite early times, the development of popular preaching dates from the fourteenth century; and it is significant that there are few medieval pulpits in existence of earlier date. Theological subtlety was not particularly encouraged among parish parsons, and the later village sermon would probably be a cheerful and informal discourse on the moralities of rural life, with a vigorous strain of story-telling and humour. Of course the friars of the great preaching orders, whether they had access to the village pulpit or held their services in the open air, latterly attracted crowds from miles around, for their verbal fireworks were famous, and might even provide a counter-attraction to a country fair. But these friars were anything but popular with the parish priests, with whose duties they often interfered and whose authority they tended to undermine.

If a daily attendance at Mass was fairly usual, the average layman would only rarely partake of the Sacrament, though the Easter Communion was practically universal. While more frequent penance was increasingly urged from the pulpits as the Middle Ages advanced, it remained the custom for all and sundry to flock to their shriving during Holy Week, an inconvenient practice that often called for the hire of additional chaplains. During the earlier Middle Ages at least, no regular seating was probably supplied in the nave except for an occasional stone bench around the base of a pillar or in the arcade of a wall; later, with the development of carpentry, wooden pews and benches, often of some elaboration, were provided, and even sometimes leased to parishioners in order of social precedence—another useful source of revenue. Social distinctions, it may be added, were latterly as rigidly maintained in church as out of it, especially where the feminine element was concerned. The question of priority in the Sunday distribution of the "holy loaf" after Mass occasionally led to undignified brawls, and Langland describes a savage scrap between ladies over precedence in taking this bread—after church, of course. By the fifteenth century, the local lord was generally boxed up in his private pew or chapel (though the women were first 'y parroked in puwes'), and in the country few priests would venture to begin the service without him.

It is only possible to touch briefly on the varied round of ritual for saints' days and festivals, which must generally have been of a moving beauty. Holy Week was an almost continuous pageant beginning with the branch-bearing and chants of the Palm Sunday procession, with its dramatic last station at the shrouded Rood, through the *Tenebrae* of Wednesday and Sheer Thursday, when the priest washed the feet of the poor, to the vigil of Good Friday, with its solemn "Creeping to the Cross." Throughout Lent a great white veil hung between the nave and chancel, and the crosses and images were shrouded with white cloths, generally marked with the red St. George's cross that was such a feature of the English ritual. Holy Saturday saw the blessing of the Paschal Candle, and Easter Sunday was ushered in triumphantly with vast corporate Communions and the solemn transference of the Host and Crucifix from the Easter Sepulchre to the high altar.

A curious and interesting ceremony was the so-called Childermass, celebrated on St. Nicholas' Day in many churches by a band of children, with a boy-bishop at their head, who might afterwards preach a sermon. Miracle plays—solemn and bucolic representations of Old and New Testament scenes by village people or itinerant players—were frequently staged in the aisles of churches, or, where they existed, in parish halls. The feast of the patron saint of the building would be celebrated as a parish holiday, and this often degenerated by stages into quite a considerable churchyard fair, with booths, dancing and amusements. Other diversions included parish ales—eating and drinking beanfeasts organised to raise funds, which might be held in a church nave or parish hall—and morris dancing.

The use of the nave for these festivities must have tinged with affection the veneration and respect felt by all for the church fabric. For its parishioners it was the centre of life in every province, solemn or gay, and the symbol of their hopes for eternity. Here a child would be brought to its baptism a few hours after birth; here it would be taught the Creed and the Commandments by the parish clerk; and here it would first receive the benefits of the Sacrament. Here a man was welcomed into matrimony in the porch, and nearby in the churchyard his body was lowered into the grave to the slow beat of the parish bell. In the measured ceremonial of Anglican observance, it is sometimes difficult nowadays to visualise the same fabric in the gleam and glow of its old decoration, its walls bright with coloured cartoons and diapers, its shadows pricked with the flames of many candles. Contemporary literature affords us only the briefest of glimpses, as in the anonymous *Crede of Piers Plowman*, written in the difficult and stilted vulgate of the fourteenth century. For a living picture we must turn to the work of William Morris some five centuries later, who reconstructs the medieval interior with the zest of a romantic and the felicity of a poet.[1]

[1] *A Dream of John Ball.*

D

The nave was not very long, but it looked spacious too; it was somewhat old, but well-built and handsome; the roof of curved wooden rafters with great tie-beams going from wall to wall. There was no light in it but that of the moon streaming through the windows, which were by no means large, and were glazed with white fretwork, with here and there a little figure in very deep rich colours. Two larger windows near the east end of each aisle had just been made so that the church grew lighter towards the east, and I could see all the work on the great screen between the nave and chancel which glittered bright in new paint and gilding; a candle glimmered in the loft above it, before the huge Rood that filled up the whole space between the loft and the chancel-arch. There was an altar at the east end of each aisle, the one on the south side standing against the outside wall, the one on the north against a traceried gaily painted screen, for that aisle ran on along the chancel. There were a few oak benches, near this second altar, seemingly just made, and well carved and moulded; otherwise the floor of the nave, which was paved with a quaint pavement of glazed tiles like the crocks I had seen outside as to ware, was quite clear, and the shafts of the arches rose out of it white and beautiful under the moon as though out of a sea, dark but with gleams struck over it. . . .

* * *

The ethics of the great spiritual movement that we call the Reformation are outside the province of this chapter; there is no doubt, however, that the covetousness and laxity of the clergy during the fifteenth century had done much to undermine their prestige in the public eye, while the effeteness of monasticism had been a persistent scandal for a hundred years and more. Henry VIII's personal quarrel brought to a head a rankling public dissatisfaction with a corrupt Papacy and its agents, and the movement towards reform was so spontaneous and vigorous in its beginnings that the first iconoclastic excesses, if not to be approved, can certainly be understood. It must also be remembered that, throughout the religious changes of the sixteenth century, the easy-going tolerance of the main body of Englishmen, who accepted the Reformation without scruples, was continually inflamed by the extreme doctrinal religionists who formed a spearhead of the left, poised to strike deep into the heart of traditional Catholicism. Another factor was the rapacity of the king and his officials, who roamed the country like jackals at this time, feeding on the spoils of the prostrate Church.

The spoliation of the monasteries was quickly followed by an attack on the parish churches. Most of these were by now very rich in their appointments, their treasures in plate alone

17 WALPOLE ST. PETER, NORFOLK: The Fifteenth-century Interior of a great Marshland Church (*vide* also fig. 29)

19 ST. THOMAS OF CANTERBURY, SALISBURY ;
The Aisle Chapel of a fine Town Church

18 MULLION, CORNWALL: A typical Interior of
the District, with modern Rood and Loft

often exceeding those of a modern cathedral. In their determination to eradicate all that breathed of superstition, Edward VI's Commissioners directed a particularly fierce onslaught on the carved roods or crucifixes that surmounted the screens of every parish church beneath the chancel-arch, with figures of the Virgin and St. John on either hand;[1] and so thorough were their methods that not a single example remains *in situ*, and a grand legacy of English carving has vanished. Many such roods, together with cheaper substitutes for the images, vestments and equipment destroyed, were temporarily set up again during the Marian Reaction of 1553–58; at Ludham in Norfolk, for instance, the rood was replaced at this time by a painting of the Crucifixion on boards, surmounting the old rood-beam and completely filling the head of the chancel arch, which is still in place. Such a makeshift is probably explained by local scepticism as to the stability of the revived *régime*.

The churchwardens' accounts of this tumultuous quarter-century sometimes tell a graphic story. Thus, at St. Martin's at Leicester in 1545–46, there is an entry recording the sale of the whole church plate to "Mr. tallance then maire of covētre" for the considerable sum of £24 5s. 10d., while during the next two years the sale of vestments and fittings to various townsmen realised as much as £25 5s. 5d. It is of interest that after one of these sales a sum of over £9 was divided among a long list of poor people in the parish. Frequent items now appear such as the 1s. 8d. paid to "Robert Sextin and his fellow ffor takyng downe tabernacles & Images," and the 1s. 6d. to "John Wynterscale, Robert Sekerston & Roger Johnson for takyng downe the Rode loft." In 1553–54, however, the same Robert Sekerston earned a further 1s. for "settyng upp the alter and mendyng of the churche," and throughout Mary's reign there were innumerable small charges for the restoration of vestments and fittings, generally on a fairly modest scale, such as the 1s. 4d. paid for "a yarde & a quarte of red sey to Cover the canopy over the Sacrament," 2s. 6d. for "a pyx for the Sacrament," 1s. 1d. to "John barbers wyffe for gyldyng the rode mary and Iohn," and 1s. 4d. to "Nichis lawson for a pattyn of the Challyce." In 1558, 8d. was paid out "for ale to the Ryngers when the quenes grace was pclamyd"—from which time events began to move rapidly. In the same year, more ale to the value of 3d. was consumed by the four men engaged on "tayken downe the altar stones," and there were items for "a bible & a para-

[1] A recent reconstruction is illustrated on Fig. 18.

phrasis," a "sarvis boke," and an "Iniunction boke." In 1561, 1s. 1d. was paid to "Harre brynbyster for ye frame to ye commandments," 2s. to "Wyllam basforde for wrytyng ye ten Commandments," and 4d. to "boddeley for takyng up ye bordes in ye Rood larfe." The climax was reached in 1570–71, however, when 1s. 8d. was paid "unto yreland for cuttynge downe the ymages hedes in the churche," and 1s. "unto Wylyame symsoune and robert craftes for takynge downe ye thynge over ye funt."

Nevertheless, Elizabeth's firm rule brought an element of order and logic into the work of destruction. Thus, in the third year of her reign, came "A Proclamation against breaking or defacing of Monuments of Antiquitie, being set up in Churches, or other publike places, for memory, and not for superstition." This was directed against the more extreme reforming elements, who were straitly forbidden to "breake downe or deface any image in glasse-windowes in any Church, without consent of the Ordinary: upon paine that whosoever shal herein be found to offend, to be committed to the next Goale, and there to remain without baile or mainprise unto the next comming of the Iustices, for the delivery of the said Goale." In his *Description of England*, published in 1577, William Harrison, himself a clergyman, remarked that in the "churches themselves, belles and times of morning & evening praier remain as in time past, saving that all images, shrines, tabernacles, rood loftes & monuments of idolatrie are removed, taken down & defaced: Onlie the stories in glasse windowes excepted, which, for want of sufficient store of new stuffe, and by reason of extreame charge that should grow by the alteration of the same into white panes throughoute the realme, are not altogether abolished in most places at once, but by little and little suffered to decaie that white glass may be set up in their roomes." The antiquarian spirit had still to be born, even in the English Golden Age.

The next reign brought some little activity in church furnishing; carved pulpits, communion tables, chairs, pews, and even screens, charged with the fashionable motives of the Flemish pattern-books, were now introduced where there was money to spend, and remain to this day, very beautiful and complete in certain churches such as Croscombe in Somerset (20) and St. John's at Leeds. The High Church reaction under the Stuarts was followed by a brief return of ritual beauty in the arrangement and appointment of many churches; and though much of this was swept away angrily in the disorders of the Interregnum, a little remains to testify to the taste and discrimination of prelates such as Laud, Hacket, Cosin and their agents, as in the fine woodwork installed by the latter bishop in some parish churches of the Durham Diocese. The release of rabid puritan elements under the Commonwealth, however, brought a recrudescence of the old smashing spirit. Now the uprooting of superstition was not considered enough; the whole range of religious representation was attacked, and the conception of a devotional implication in the church fabric condemned. A vast body of medieval craftsmanship that had survived the Reformation was now summarily destroyed by Parliamentary troops and sympathisers, including much of the great English heritage of stained glass, hitherto largely spared, which was now so efficiently despatched by fanatics of the type of Dowsing, the "parliamentary visitor" of the Suffolk and Cambridge churches, that little remains in this country, except in fragments, of a grand medieval art.

Throughout the seventeenth and eighteenth centuries, at least so far as the fabrics were concerned, the parish churches were left in the peace of semi-stagnation, their architectural beauty ignored and little care given to their preservation beyond the bare necessities of maintenance. With the nineteenth, as is well known, came a genuine, if often busy and misdirected, revival of interest, and a wide activity in restoration, which, in spite of its sometimes lamentable consequences, did undoubtedly preserve many buildings from otherwise inevitable ruin. For all its encaustic tiles and pitch pine, its sentimental glass and gasoliers, the Victorian Age produced a body of ecclesiological scholarship and research to which must be attributed much of the better understanding of our own times. Now, though the straitness of Church finances often limits the scope of maintenance and repair, we may be sure that pretentious ignorance will not be tolerated in work on these buildings, while the affection and sentiment of an informed public are the best modern safeguards against their decay.

* * *

It only remains to sketch briefly the manner in which the cure of souls has been maintained under the aegis of the developed *Ecclesia Anglicana* from the Reformation to our own times. It was the misfortune of the new Church that, beyond its birthright of a revised doctrine and an incomparable liturgy, it had to inherit many of the abuses and much of the obsolete administrative machinery of the old order—though the parish, with its "vestry" committee and churchwardens, became an important unit in Tudor local government. With the consolidation of Church discipline under Elizabeth, the wardens became virtually the ecclesiastical magistrates of their parishes, levying their rates for fabric maintenance, providing the books and equipment prescribed by the Royal Injunctions, and reporting delinquents to the biennial archdeacon's court. Churchgoing was enforced by law, and a comfortable income often derived in fines from local recusants and offenders. The forms of the services were somewhat as they are to-day, though the times were earlier; and the puritan tinge can be observed in the extraordinary popularity of preaching—which reached its zenith some quarter of a century later with the metaphysical thunders of John Donne—and in the circulation of ingenuous manuals of devotion under such titles as *The Sinful Man's Solace* and *The Pomander of Prayer*.

After the Restoration, English churchmanship settled down to a long phase of quiescent mediocrity that was to endure for almost two centuries. The Georgian period saw a recrudescence of perhaps the worst abuse of the pre-Reformation Church—that of absenteeism—the cure of souls being now largely relegated to a throng of dejected starveling curates, lucky if they earned their meagre £40 a year, while the holders of the benefices were, as often as not, enabled to pursue the careers of their choice in the great world of affairs. It is true that to the comparative leisure afforded by this system we owe the works of a Swift, a Sterne, a Crabbe, and a White of Selborne; but it can hardly be denied that the English Church failed in its mission at a critical point in its development, when a new order was taking shape beneath its eyes, largely leaving to John Wesley and his followers the great tasks of spiritual enlightenment and evangelisation in the growing industrial centres and in the New World.

Sunday service in the eighteenth-century village church can seldom, indeed, have been very inspiring. In the first place, it would be generally without music—a droning duet between the parson and the clerk—though occasionally enlivened by the melody of a barrel-organ or the fiddles and serpents of a gallery band. The squire's progress up the aisle would be attended by the bows and curtseys of the congregation; once boxed in his pew, with its scarlet hassocks and blazing fire in winter, the service could proceed, reaching its culmination in the drowsy periods of a long sermon of unimpeachable orthodoxy, worked up perhaps from the published homilies of some popular Georgian divine. Immediately after service,

20 CROSCOMBE, SOMERSET: The Interior, with its range of Jacobean Fittings

21 AVINGTON, HAMPSHIRE: An Unspoilt Church Interior of the
English Renaissance

the curate might take horse and make his way through the winter slough of the countryside to a sister parish several miles off for an early Evensong—so at least we see him, drooping over his lean steed, in Dighton's caricature. It is hardly surprising that such conditions produced the obsequious and spiritless breed of parson condemned by Crabbe:

> Content to bow, be silent and obey,
> And by a soothing suff'rance find his way. . . .

The full-blooded zest for a life of so human a figure as Parson Woodforde—who incidentally had an income of his own— comes as a relief; though Woodforde, always conscientious if seldom transcendent in his duties, was a model of propriety compared with some of the "sporting parsons" of the Regency who have come down to us in lampoon and caricature, such as the formidable Mr. Chowne of Exmoor, the likeable Jack Russell, who preached in hunting boots and a cassock, and, in Leicestershire, little "Spurting" Bullen who hunted all his fifty-four years at Eastwell, and Storey of Lockington who staged a cock-fight in his church with the Marquis of Hastings. At the same time, the better type of clergyman was never wanting; there is ample evidence that Goldsmith's Vicar of Wakefield had his frequent parallels, as, at Stoney Stanton in Leicestershire, in John Bold, whose ministrations transformed the parish, and who, out of his stipend of £30, left no less than £240 to his friends and the poor. Baring Gould has quoted a delightful parson's epitaph from his own church at Lew Trenchard in Devon, which must have characterised many an incumbent at this period. It concludes:

> He servèd God devout: and strived men's souls to save.
> He fedd the poore, lov'd all, and did by Pattern showe
> As pastor to his Flocke, ye way that they shoulde go.

Throughout the nineteenth century, English churchmanship steered a middle course between the spiritual peaks of the Oxford Movement and the Evangelical Revival. With the rise in population consequent on Industrialisation came an outburst of church building, first Classic, then under the impetus of the Gothic Revival; and the appearance of vast new urban parishes of working and "middling" people called for, and generally produced, a more active and useful type of parson, capable of bearing the heavier burden of duties demanded. At the same time, the routine of country parishes was little affected, and family and college livings continued to be filled from the ranks of younger sons and retired dons respectively, who served them conscientiously enough, if often without great exertion. But the standard of the ministry was undoubtedly much higher than in the previous century, and it must not be forgotten that no mean proportion of the scholarship and minor literature of the Victorian Age was the product of country parsonages. Another feature of these pleasant homes was the large families they sponsored of healthy active children, who formed a willing stream of recruitment for the expanding outposts of the Empire and the young Dominions. It is a fact that hundreds of rectories were enlarged in the 'fifties and 'sixties of the last century, often to the great inconvenience of their later occupants.

Services were now everywhere conducted with more reverence and dignity, and the latter part of the century saw a marked revival in congregational music. The spiritual life of the English eighteenth and nineteenth centuries is well expressed in its hymnody, which, when separated from much mawkishness, represents a really impressive achievement in music and verse. With the return of chanted and choral services came a gathering up of psalm-chants and anthems from many sources—ranging from Purcell to Beethoven and back from Sullivan to Arne. These, with the majestic poetry of the liturgy, bring an added beauty and inspiration to the Anglican service which makes it dear to most Englishmen, whether heard in the vast spaces of a cathedral or in the ancient intimacy of a parish church.

PUDDLETOWN, DORSET
Drawn by W. Curtis Green, R.A.

22 WEDMORE, SOMERSET: A Fifteenth-century Interior of
West Country Non-Clerestoreyed Type

23 WHITBY, YORKSHIRE: A Georgian Interior with the "Three-decker"
Pulpit arrangement

24 WITNEY, OXFORDSHIRE: The Thirteenth-century Tower Crossing and
Chancel. Note the typical Lancets of the East End

CHAPTER TWO

The Evolution of the Parish Church:
the Arrangement and Planning

THIS chapter will begin with a short summary of the development of parish church planning through the Middle Ages, forming a basis for subsequent discussion and elaboration. It was a process open to such wide variation that it is often difficult to differentiate the rule from the exception; but it is well to keep in mind from the first that nearly all parish church plans may ultimately be traced back to one of three fundamental types in use during the twelfth century. These were:

1. The Nave and Sanctuary (Two-cell Type).
2. The Nave, Chancel, and Sanctuary (Three-cell Type).
3. The Cruciform or Cross Church, with Nave, Transepts, Sanctuary and Central Tower.

Type 2 did not continue as a permanent form, but instances of it occur about the country, and there are cases of rebuilding as late as the fourteenth century, as at Biddestone in Wiltshire and Etchingham in Sussex. A fourth type, the Circular Plan, need scarcely be considered, for of it only five examples remain, mostly built for one of the military orders: St. Sepulchre's at Northampton, the Temple Church in London, the Holy Sepulchre at Cambridge, Little Maplestead in Essex, and the Chapel of Ludlow Castle.

There is a cogent reason for referring these three types back to the twelfth century. The Norman conquest of England resulted, after a lapse of some forty years, in a wave of church building all over the country. Almost all the pre-Conquest churches, particularly those built of wood, were reconstructed, and many others of fresh ecclesiastical foundation arose on the manors of the new Norman lords. While few escaped the transforming zeal of the builders, churches are still to be found throughout the country in which the main fabric is definitely pre-Conquest in date, though the majority have been much added to or altered. These for the most part belong to the first two types, as Escomb in Durham for Type 1, and Barton-on-Humber in Lincolnshire for Type 2, the latter originally with a middle nave-tower between a narthex and small eastern sanctuary. Examples are also to be found with one or more transept arms, as Breamore in Hampshire (43) and Bradford-on-Avon in Wiltshire (26). Worth in Sussex has boldly defined transepts and an apsidal sanctuary—the latter a rare feature in a pre-Conquest church. But to show something of the variety that must have existed among larger buildings, it is only necessary to examine the venerable church of Brixworth near Northampton, which reveals an original aisled nave (25) with an arcade of Roman tiles (now filled in with later windows), and an eastern apse above a crypt ambulatory. Pre-Conquest crypts also occur at Wing in Buckinghamshire and Repton in Derbyshire.

The revival of church building that followed the Conquest was accompanied by a fairly general adherence to the forms of Types 1 and 2 for ordinary parish churches, which were built either square-ended, as at Elkstone (54), or apsidal, as at Hales in Norfolk (32) and Kilpeck in Herefordshire. Type 1 was often further elaborated by the addition of a western tower in place of a bellcote (or small bell-turret raised over the western gable); or sometimes the nave was built with aisles but without a tower. It is rare to find a twelfth-century church of this type planned in the first instance with both these features.

The simplest form of Type 3 was a church with aisleless nave, square-planned transepts and simple sanctuary, with a lantern-tower over the crossing, as at Old Shoreham in Sussex (42). Such a building might also have a square or apsidal chapel on the east side of each transept arm. These chapels have almost invariably disappeared, but the thirteenth-century cross church at Uffington in Berkshire retains an interesting pair, square-ended, in the north transept, and a single one in the south (33). An aisled nave is occasionally found in this type, but the parish churches of the twelfth century were seldom provided with porches.

The cruciform plan carries with it some obvious disadvantages. Thus, the massive piers indispensable for supporting a central tower obstruct space, view and sound in the heart of the church (24), and in aisleless examples the transepts are entirely secluded from the main body of the building. Consequently, this plan was never of very general adoption for parish purposes, though it is of obstinate recurrence down to a late date, either singly or in groups, in most parts of the country.

It is thus from Types 1 and 3 that the more complex plan of later times has chiefly evolved. Naves have received the addition of aisles, clerestories and porches, the latter often

25 BRIXWORTH, NORTHAMPTONSHIRE : An ambitious Saxon
Interior.   The Arcade has been built up

26 BRADFORD-ON-AVON, WILTSHIRE : The Saxon Chapel from the
North-west, and the North Transept

27 THE HEATH CHAPEL, SHROPSHIRE: An untouched Norman
Building in remote Country

28 STEWKLEY, BUCKINGHAMSHIRE: The Norman Nave
and Central Tower

of two storeys, while the chancel itself has been lengthened or rebuilt, sometimes with aisles and even a clerestory. Large chapels replace the small early ones of the transepts; new towers have been added, existing ones heightened, or, in cross churches, the central tower replaced by another at the west end, as at St. Cuthbert's at Wells (38). The transepts themselves have become merged in the aisles, or else have been extended and rebuilt, in rare instances with aisles of their own. Further additions include sacristies, crypts and chantry chapels, the latter in a variety of positions, sometimes even, as at Gaddesby in Leicestershire, at the west end.

Many such changes might occur in the structural history of

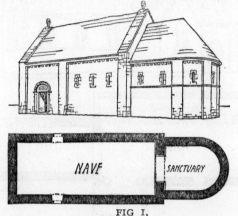

FIG I.
The original twelfth-century apsidal building
(*This series of 5 Plans is reproduced uniformly to a scale of 36 feet to 1 inch*)

a parish church in its development through the medieval centuries. In other cases, while fulfilling its parish functions without interruption, the fabric may have undergone little or no change beyond the occasional alteration of a window, a doorway, or an arch. Some churches, again, have only partly developed, throwing out, perhaps, an aisle and a chapel, while others, with the growth in prosperity of their neighbourhoods, have been almost totally rebuilt, and only provide the slenderest evidence of their original forms. Such rebuildings, however, were generally carried through piecemeal, so that the church might remain in constant use. As a result, there is invariably some indication, however slight, of the design of the earlier church, the original arrangement of which can generally be traced.

To illustrate these points, a series of comparative plans and perspective views has been included. These do not illustrate any specific church, or profess to record every variety of addition. They are rather intended to show the average process of change and development in the typical church of a prosperous town parish from the twelfth century to the close of the medieval period, and in every case the features noted are paralleled by actual examples, and the development follows a sequence in line with changing social conditions and the requirements of medieval ritual.

Fig. I illustrates the church as it would have been built,

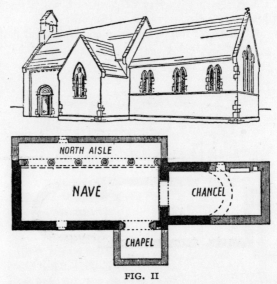

FIG. II

Thirteenth-century additions: aisle, chapel and new chancel
(*For explanation of hatching v. Fig. V*)

or rebuilt, in the twelfth century, and this fundamental plan is shown dotted through every subsequent development. With the thirteenth century, an enlargement would be necessary of this modest little building, consisting originally of an aisleless nave and apsidal sanctuary. A north aisle would be added for the accommodation of the growing congregation, the apse being removed and the sanctuary lengthened into a chancel. On the south side of the nave a rich benefactor has now built and endowed a transeptal chantry chapel, in connection with which a gild has been formed (Fig. II).

With the fourteenth century this gild has increased in importance, and its chapel has been extended into a full south aisle. At the same time, the north aisle has been widened to allow more altar-space for the congregation. A north porch has been built at the same period, a sacristy added to the chancel, and the twelfth-century chancel arch replaced by a wider one (Fig. III).

With the fifteenth century, the original gild, now very rich, has undertaken the rebuilding of its south aisle, adding a two-storeyed porch and reconstructing the south arcade. A later gild has built a north chapel on to the chancel, and a rich donor has presented a screen with loft and rood,

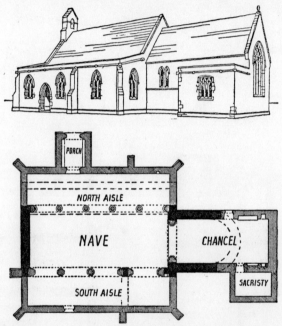

FIG. III

The fourteenth-century contribution: new aisles, porch, sacristy, etc.

altering the chancel arch for the purpose, and cutting a rood staircase in the masonry. The parish has undertaken the building of a new western tower, the work being carried out to cause the minimum interference with the use of the nave. This, when high enough to roof in, would be opened into the church by the removal of the original twelfth-century west wall (Fig. IV).

Towards the close of the fifteenth century, a third gild has undertaken the building of a south chapel to the chancel, a small sacristy having already been placed at its south-east corner. With this operation might go the addition of a chancel clerestory. A merchant of the town has provided a stately north porch with a chamber over it. At the same time, the thirteenth-century walling over the nave arcade has been found faulty from age, leaning outwards, perhaps, with the roof thrust, and has been rebuilt in the current fashion,

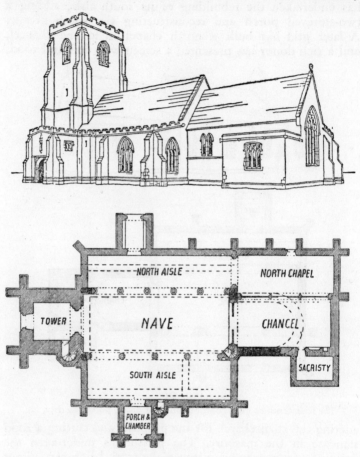

FIG. IV

Early fifteenth-century extensions: tower, porch, nave and chancel aisles, etc.

with a clerestory. Finally, the tower has been raised to its full height and received its peal of bells (Fig. V).

Throughout this church's history, then, the external width and length of the old nave, the width of the chancel, and until the last period of growth, the height of the walls have been the determining factors in its development. The nave and chancel have only been widened by the piercing of their

29 WALPOLE ST. PETER, NORFOLK: The Exterior from the South (*vide* also fig. 17)

30 ST. JOHN'S, DEVIZES, WILTSHIRE : The stern Norman of the East
End contrasted with the rich Perpendicular of its South Chapel

side walls with arcades opening on to aisles, the nave has been
lengthened only by the addition of the western tower, and the
building only heightened by clerestories. In its final phase,

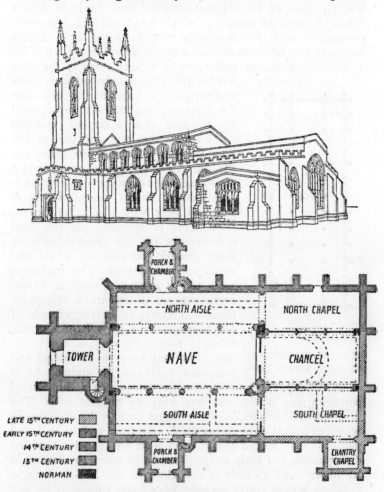

FIG. V

The late fifteenth-century final transformation: clerestory, chapels, etc.

practically nothing of the original fabric has remained above
ground; only the angle quoin may be traced under the plaster
of the north-east chapel, the rood-staircase having largely
eliminated the south-east one, and the western ones being
encased in the masonry of the tower. But for all that, it is
obvious that the original church has to some extent dictated

the form of the building throughout its history, and that the earlier additions have similarly influenced the later ones.

After such a transformation, the church may well have lost all trace of its original confined and dimly lit aspect caused by narrow openings, small windows, and a massive treatment; with its dominant window areas and slender supports the effect is now essentially graceful and airy. Its very conception has undergone a radical change; the plan has been simplified on broad lines, walls and supports reduced to the minimum for stability, and the interior opened up to give that sense of tranquil spaciousness that was the aim of the later English builders. Throughout the Middle Ages, we can watch this aim maturing in the development of church architecture, almost unconsciously at first but later with a steadfast intention. This is apparent in the final enlargement of the chancel arch in many greater churches, or in its disappearance altogether. The buildings were now conceived purely as stonework lanterns of rich and lovely polychrome glazing, as in the church of St. Nicholas at King's Lynn, which, though nominally only a chapel-of-ease, has long been to all intents and purposes parochial in status. As it stands to-day, this building has developed into a three-aisled parallelogram, about 162 feet long by 70 feet wide. The division of the interior was effected entirely by screenwork which extended right across the church from wall to wall, and probably also fenced the chancel from its chapels. This has disappeared, but little imagination is required to picture, in its beauty and mystery at the close of the Middle Ages, a building which could scarcely have been surpassed by any church in England, though founded on the strictest simplicity of plan.

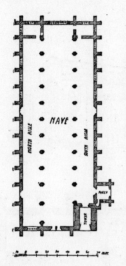

PLAN OF ST. NICHOLAS' CHURCH, KING'S LYNN

* * *

This summary has attempted to indicate the broad lines of development in a typical though hypothetical instance subjected to the maximum of alteration and addition. It now remains to examine in more detail the three fundamental types

31   IPPLEPEN, DEVON: A Typical later Interior of this District, without Chancel Arch, but with rich carving and a continuous Screen

32 HALES, NORFOLK: Built of the local Flint, with Norman Apse,
Round Tower and Thatch

33 UFFINGTON, BERKSHIRE: The Octagonal Tower, Early English
South Transept with its Chapel

defined at the beginning of the chapter, and to consider their numerous variations and combinations. This is a large subject which cannot be treated as adequately as it deserves, and has never received the attention at the hands of investigators that its importance warrants.

After the conversion of Saxon England, the plans of the first Christian churches were, as has been seen, fairly varied, though mostly conforming to the two-cell nave and sanctuary arrangement of Type 1, generally without apse. This feature, where it appeared, was mostly confined to the South-East, as at Worth in Sussex and Reculver in Kent—a fact that has sometimes, though possibly with small justification, connected its use with the missionary activities of St. Augustine of Canterbury and his successors. Saxon apses were either semicircular, as at Worth, or polygonal, as at Wing in Buckinghamshire. But by far the greater number of these churches seem to have been built with the rectangular east end so characteristic of English methods, whether deriving, as some writers have suggested, from the stone cell-chapels of the Celtic missionaries, from an old timber tradition of Northern Europe, or from cultural connections with Rhenish monasticism.

Little except castles and monasteries was built in the period of suspension immediately following the Conquest, and it was not until the beginning of the twelfth century that the new landowners set themselves with vigour to build or reconstruct churches of every sort and size throughout the country in their own version of Romanesque. From the great monastic establishments such as Durham, Winchester, and Norwich to the hamlet chapels of fen and wold, England has perhaps never experienced so brisk a building activity in a technique imposed by the conquerors and quickly assimilated and adapted by the subject people. With the comparatively thin and scattered population of the country at this time, it is a fact of some significance that the number of parish churches at the compilation of Domesday Book seems practically to have equalled that at the close of the eighteenth century, on the threshold of the Industrial Revolution.

The new technique brought, naturally enough, a revival of the apse, which still appeared in the largest numbers in South-Eastern and Eastern England. Typical examples of its use in country churches can be seen at Steetley in Derbyshire, Nateley Scures in Hampshire, Kilpeck in Herefordshire, and Hales in Norfolk (32); Newhaven in Sussex is the only case in which it projects from a central chancel-tower—the sailors,

F

to whom it is a landmark, say, "Newhaven Church sails stern first." At the same time, the English tradition of the square-ended church persisted unobtrusively in most districts, and is to be found in such far-removed examples as Stewkley in Buckinghamshire (28), Adel in Yorkshire, Elkstone in the Cotswolds (54), and Studland in Dorset.

While smaller Norman churches occasionally consisted of a single compartment only, as at Nateley Scures in Hampshire and Little Tey in Essex, the threefold division of Type 2 is also characteristic. Type 1 is likewise of frequent occurrence, and at least one example of a four-cell church survives at Peterchurch in Herefordshire. This arrangement, however, must always have been exceptional. The chancel is sometimes formed by the space under a central tower; in other cases, the central tower may be either wider or narrower than the chancel adjoining, as at Coln St. Denis in Gloucestershire and Bredon in Worcestershire respectively. Smaller Norman churches were often built on a plan which gave the nave exactly double the length of the sanctuary, and the height of the compartments sometimes precisely equalled their width.

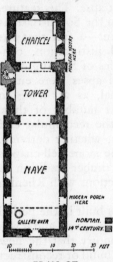

PLAN OF
STEWKLEY CHURCH,
BUCKINGHAMSHIRE

The number and beauty of Norman arcades in existence are evidence of the early if restricted use of the aisled nave, not unknown in Saxon architecture; among twelfth-century examples on a grand scale are Melbourne in Derbyshire (56), and Walsoken and Tilney All Saints in Norfolk. When more accommodation was needed in an aisleless nave, it was generally procured by throwing out an aisle on the north side, an addition occasionally made during the twelfth but more characteristic of the thirteenth century. The reason for the choice of this side was fairly obvious. The Normans as a rule made their chief entrances on the south, enriched with carving and occasionally with a shallow porch. There was also a strong feeling against burial on the north side of the church, so that the ground here was unencumbered by graves and thus suitable for an extension. A south aisle, of course, generally followed in due course, but many examples exist,

34 TILNEY ALL SAINTS, NORFOLK : The Perpendicular casing of a Norman Nave

35　LAVENHAM, SUFFOLK : The Late-Fifteenth Century Interior of a
great " Wool " Church

36　STRATFORD-ON-AVON, WARWICKSHIRE : A Light-filled Chancel of the
Fifteenth Century.　Shakespeare's Monument is to the left of the Table Tomb

of which Little Munden in Hertfordshire is one, in which a north aisle alone has been added. Very occasionally a solitary south aisle is found, as in a group of churches in the Isle of Wight that includes Carisbrooke (*frontispiece*); in these its breadth often nearly, if not quite, equals that of the nave.

All medieval extensions were contrived to cause the minimum disturbance of the daily use of the fabric. In the case of aisle additions, the new exterior walls were first raised on the outside and covered with a sloping roof. A gap was left to serve as the entrance, and to this the old nave doorway was often bodily removed, to cause curious problems of dating for later generations. The next stage was to build up the piers of the arcade in gaps made for the purpose in the old walls, after which further breaches were cut for the arch voussoirs. The under parts that had served as arch-centerings were then removed, and the new aisles thrown into the church.

Hence, the walling above the arcade is frequently the oldest part of the fabric, and is sometimes even of pre-Conquest date. In it the outlines of the old nave windows can occasionally be traced, perhaps cut into by the springing of the arcade. Compton Martin in Somerset can show a Norman clerestory above the south arcade, now surmounted by the roof of a later and higher aisle. A rough and ready measure was to dispense with specially built piers and leave the arches supported by solid blocks of the old nave walling, as at Ickham and Chislet in Kent. If it was decided to widen or heighten an existing aisle, the same methods were usually followed.

THE CLERESTORY

When the builders began to throw out aisles, they were faced with problems of lighting that were to recur throughout the medieval period. The solution of these problems was most effectively found in the construction of a clerestory. It may be well at this juncture to deal briefly by anticipation with this feature, which is also referred to later on.

The simplest method of roofing a newly added aisle was to continue the slope of the nave roof at the same angle, as is so often found in Sussex churches. In a type characteristic of the fourteenth century, the aisle roof was given a flattish pitch, springing from the base of the nave roof and thus precluding a clerestory, though compensating window space was provided in the comparatively lofty aisle wall. An alternative method was to gable the aisles to the same height as the nave, bringing about the "three-gable" arrangement so favoured by

the fourteenth- and fifteenth-century builders in Devon, Cornwall, and sometimes in Kent. Occasionally, also, a chancel
chapel had its separate gable, as at Shere, Merstham (124), and
Chaldon in Surrey. But by far the simplest solution of the
lighting problem was to heighten the walls above the arcade
and pierce them with windows; in a word, to build a clerestory.
To this, a steep-pitched roof was at first generally attached, but
with the fifteenth century, from which most clerestories date,
a flattish roof masked by a parapet became almost invariable,
except in East Anglia, where traditions always seemed to die
hardest. Such a roof would be almost without thrust on the
thin clerestory walls, the battlements, parapets and pinnacles
being chiefly a decorative expedient to break the skyline.

Clerestories were raised not only over naves but over
chancels, particularly those with aisle chapels, as at Tilney
All Saints in Norfolk (34). In many large and fully developed
churches of the Eastern Counties, the clerestory is continuous
over nave and chancel in an unbroken line, as at Southwold,
Blythburgh and Lowestoft. More often, however, the nave
alone is clerestoried, the chancel sometimes retaining its original
roof of steep pitch (130).

Churches exist in which the clerestory is an original Norman
or Transitional feature, but these, if cathedrals and minsters
are excluded, are comparatively rare. Examples can be seen
at Filey in Yorkshire, Compton Martin in Somerset and St.
Margaret-at-Cliffe in Kent. The clerestory became commoner
during the thirteenth century, as at Elm in Cambridgeshire,
Aymestry in Herefordshire, Darlington, Horsham, and elsewhere, and by the fourteenth century was a familiar feature,
the window openings, however, being still comparatively
small, though enriched with delicate Geometrical or Curvilinear tracery. With the fifteenth century, the advances made
in glass-painting and the popularity of donors' and memorial
windows brought about a new conception of this feature;
and towards the close of the century it was common to find the
upper walls presenting an almost greater area of glass than
of stone, as in a whole range of splendid later churches such
as Lavenham (72), St. Mary's, Bury St. Edmunds (40), and
Long Melford (74) in Suffolk, Gedney, Boston and Holbeach in
Lincolnshire, Chipping Norton in Oxfordshire and many others.

Occasionally, clerestories are found in aisleless churches,
forming a second tier of nave windows, as at Sandiacre and
Wilne in Derbyshire, and Halford and Ilmington in Warwickshire. It is almost certain that in such cases an aisle or
aisles were contemplated but never built. A freak arrange-

37 TERRINGTON ST. CLEMENT, NORFOLK : A vast Perpendicular Church rising majestically above the Marshes

38 ST. CUTHBERT'S, WELLS, SOMERSET : A stately Fifteenth-century Reconstruction, with one of the finest towers of the West Country (*vide* also fig. 49)

39 SAFFRON WALDEN, ESSEX : A spacious Late-Perpendicular Interior from the South Aisle

40   ST. MARY'S, BURY ST. EDMUNDS, SUFFOLK: Showing the continuous window ranges
of the **Fifteenth-century Aisles and Clerestory**

ment is a second tier of windows in the aisle walls, as at Broughton in Oxfordshire.

THE LATER DEVELOPMENT OF THE PLAN

Before passing on to later phases, it cannot be too strongly emphasised that the Norman plan, either simple or cruciform, represented a perfectly consistent development in itself, thoroughly in accordance with early liturgical requirements. When the opportunity arose to build on a grand scale it was eagerly taken, as can be realised from such stately parochial examples as Walsoken in Norfolk and Melbourne in Derbyshire (56). But, as has been seen, the meagreness of the population made this only possible in exceptional cases; the majority of parish churches were of modest dimensions, and the processes of enlargement that began with the thirteenth century were the result of increasing congregations, and the demand for more small altars, rather than of any defect in the principle of the earlier arrangement.

The plan of the normal medieval village church, with its fairly long aisleless chancel, aisled nave, south porch, and western tower, dates principally from the later thirteenth century. Though many new churches arose at that time, it was the exception rather than the rule for them to arrive at such a point of development in a single building; first the early sanctuary would be lengthened, then the aisles added at the same or different periods, and finally the new tower built at the west end. The east ends of the aisles provided convenient positions for the new altars so badly needed; even the narrow aisles of the twelfth century had been used for this purpose, as can be seen from piscinas, almeries, and image-brackets still *in situ*. To provide this altar accommodation was often the original purpose of aisles, and instances are to be found in which they have never been completed to the full length of the nave, or else have had chapels thrown out at their east ends in the position of transepts, as is the case at Trumpington in Cambridgeshire.

Ayston in Rutland may be taken as a typical aisled parish church of the thirteenth century. Both the nave arcades were built at this period, but the north aisle is certainly slightly the older of the two—its width is 5 feet 8 inches, while the south one, probably widened at a later date, is all but three feet broader. This later widening of aisles was fairly common; there are even examples in which an aisle has been widened for only part of its length at the east end.

The accumulation of chancel chapels was a later and more gradual development. At first these were usually quite small and of chantry foundation, opening by a single arch into the chancel and by another into the aisle. Even in such an important church as Rounds in Northamptonshire there was at first only one chancel chapel, in this case connected by an arcade of three bays on the south side. Soon, however, their number and variety increased, until they finally took the form of chancel aisles, naturally producing a rectangular plan, as at Old Basing in Hampshire, and resulting in some districts in the three-gable termination already mentioned. It may be noted particularly at Launceston in Cornwall (140) and New Romney in Kent (129).

When aisles and chapels were added to cruciform churches, the projection of the transept arms generally constituted a convenient measure for their width, with the result that the transepts became merged in the general outline of the plan. The same result was also reached with chantry or gild chapels when aisles were added to a church of ordinary nave and chancel type. In both cases, the plan would take an almost, if not entirely, rectangularform, as may be seen, among many examples, at Odiham in Hampshire.

With the fourteenth century, the old constructive distinction between nave and chancel began to melt in churches of average size, as well as in larger town fabrics. Early chancel arches were rebuilt and enlarged; finally this feature tended to disappear altogether in some districts, as in Devon and Cornwall, where rood-screens achieved such elaborate forms (106), and in East Anglia, where delicately carved and painted screens abound (107). In certain instances of rebuilding, the nave and chancel division was simply maintained by a screen; in others the existing screen was moved westward to enlarge the quire. Wooden screens finally often ran right across the church from wall to wall, and were of considerable magnificence, as at Cullompton and Ipplepen (31) in Devon.

In the same way, chancel chapels were now frequently fenced by parclose screens, forming special enclosures to which the family of a founder or the members of a gild were admitted—thus becoming to all intents and purposes large pews, as at St. Saviour's Chapel at Ewelme. At Lavenham, too, there is a "pew" on each side of the church, with rich screen-work, in addition to the chapels (96). During the two centuries that preceded the Reformation, the number of chantries endowed by individuals or gilds swelled to astonishing proportions, in spite of the Statute of Mortmain, which sought to

41 LONG SUTTON, LINCOLNSHIRE: Showing the Nave, South Porch and detached
Thirteenth-century Tower, with its Lead Spire

42 OLD SHOREHAM, SUSSEX : A Norman Church built on the Cross Plan

43 BREAMORE, HAMPSHIRE : A Saxon Church with Central Tower

limit the bequests of the faithful to the Church; and the final
form of chapels was little more than that of screened enclosures,
without significance on plan. At the same time, chapels were
still occasionally added as structural features, as in the great
town churches of St. Michael and Holy Trinity at Coventry,
where they served the needs of a variety of trade gilds, including the Dyers, Cappers, Drapers, Mercers, and Tanners.
In certain larger churches, such as Cirencester and Yarmouth,
the ranges of chapels to nave or chancel were finally continuous, and resulted in an outer aisle on one or both sides.

One other feature is worth recording while on the subject
of chantry chapels. When a chancel is unaisled, no view
of the high altar is generally possible from the nave aisle-
ends or transepts. Consequently, diagonal openings called
"squints" were frequently tunnelled in the chancel-arch
piers (112) to enable chantry priests officiating at aisle or
transept altars to gain a view of the high altar. It has been
suggested that the masses at subsidiary altars tended to start
before those at the high altar, the priority of which was always
insisted upon. The squint would enable chantry priests to
synchronise their masses. In some instances, large squint
windows occur, unglazed, for the use of the congregation,
as at Burford in Oxfordshire, and similar openings are sometimes found in the nave west wall, to enable the ringer to
sound the sanctus-bell at the right moment.

THE CROSS PLAN

The long prevalent idea that the cruciform plan was deli-
berately founded upon the Cross of Christ need scarcely be
considered at the present day. Symbolism was not the aim in
these matters, and the builders' purpose was always a prac-
tical one. Similarly with the suggestion that the slight south-
ward deviation of some chancels was intended to indicate the
droop of Christ's head upon the Cross. Where this occurs,
it is probably the result of rough and ready methods of setting
out, possibly by two schools of masons working a century or
so apart.

Though a type of Saxon central tower occurs at Breamore
in Hampshire and elsewhere, the pre-Conquest builder did
not normally possess the skill to construct one on piers connected by arches. It was not until Norman methods had gained
the ascendancy just before the Conquest that the church with
transepts and a central tower supported only at its angles
came into being, as can be seen on quite a large scale at

St. Mary in the Castle at Dover. When the Normans had firmly established themselves in this country, the true cruciform plan

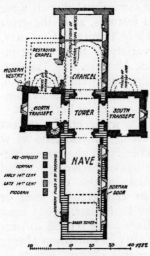

PLAN OF OLD SHOREHAM
CHURCH, SUSSEX

began to assert itself, not only in larger buildings, but in quite modest-sized parish churches. Its distribution is rather sporadic; nevertheless, Norman churches of this type are fairly numerous, as at Old Shoreham in Sussex (42), Castor in Northamptonshire, and St. John's at Devizes (30), while many others, notably in Devon and Cornwall, show traces of an original cruciform arrangement.

Some impressive cross churches with central towers arose during the thirteenth century, as at Amesbury in Wiltshire, Witney and Bampton in Oxfordshire, and Uffington in Berkshire (33); others were sometimes built with tran-

septs but without a central tower, as at Acton Burnell in Shropshire and, on a larger scale, St. Mary's at Shrewsbury and St. Mary Redcliffe, Bristol. Cruciform planning continued well into the fourteenth century, with some notable productions to its credit, such as the beautiful spire-crowned churches of Ashbourne and Chesterfield in Derbyshire. With the fifteenth century, however, when most, if not all, parishes already possessed their churches, few were built on this plan, and such as were generally replaced older cruciform structures, as at Crediton in Devon, where the Perpendicular tower is carried on the original Norman piers and arches.

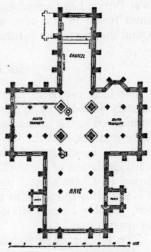

PLAN OF PATRINGTON
CHURCH, YORKSHIRE

Many cases occur in which the central tower has collapsed and been replaced by a new one at the west end, generally of fifteenth-century date, as at Tintagel in Cornwall and Kirkby

44 DOULTING, SOMERSET : A fine Cruciform Church with
Octagonal Central Tower and rich South Porch

45 PATRINGTON, YORKSHIRE : The splendid, largely Decorated Fabric from
the East, showing Transept, Lady Chapel and Perpendicular East Window
(vide also figs. 63 and 65)

Stephen in Westmorland. Examples can occasionally be found built from the first with aisles, transepts, and a western tower, as in the great churches of Rushden in Northamptonshire and Frampton and Heckington (121) in Lincolnshire, the latter two dating largely from the fourteenth century. The development fairly common in cathedrals and minsters of building aisles to the transepts also occurs in a handful of larger and more splendid parish churches, such as Patrington in Yorkshire, St. Mary Redcliffe at Bristol and Luton in Bedfordshire. In the same way, the eastern extension of the chancel to form an ambulatory or processional path, similar to the retro-quire of cathedral building, only occurs in a few very special instances in the grand manner, such as Newark in Nottinghamshire and, again, St. Mary Redcliffe at Bristol.

THE TOWER (*v.* also p. 67)

It has been seen that a tall square western tower was employed in the Saxon churches of the ninth and tenth centuries. Its primary use was to carry bells, and its form closely resembled that of the ordinary Italian *campanile.* At the same time, it could be used as a defensive refuge in times of danger, and was thus often built without a staircase, and with only minor openings in the lower stages.

It has been fairly conclusively established that the carrying up of early western narthexes or porches into towers often had a second purpose in providing a dwelling for the parish priest and others. The Saxon churches of Brixworth (25) and Deerhurst each have a window looking into the nave from quite high in the tower which could never have served a useful purpose in lighting either the church or the tower chamber, and it may be assumed that these were pierced to enable the priests to say their night offices without descending. The flues and fireplaces in the Norfolk towers of Billockby, Thornage and elsewhere may possibly have been used for baking the communion wafers, but more likely indicate a former dwelling. The large chamber in the Norman central tower of Branscombe in Devon was undoubtedly once occupied; that under the bells at Penkivel in Cornwall contains a small altar for the private use of the priest; and in at least a dozen other churches of Norman or early Gothic date there is conclusive evidence of the tower chamber having been occupied, sometimes till as late as the seventeenth century, as appears from the churchwardens' accounts of several parishes.

The west end of the nave was always the most common

G

position of the tower in England; the twin western towers of cathedral-building seldom occur in parish churches, though examples can be cited at Melbourne in Derbyshire and St. Margaret's at King's Lynn. As in every department of church architecture at this period, however, there are frequent exceptions to general usage. Norfolk, for instance, has its flanking towers on the south side, the basement serving as a porch entrance, as at Little Ellingham and Hardingham. In Cornwall, the towers of Dulse, Lawhitton and Veryan are also in this position, while that of St. Stephen-by-Saltash is at the west end of the north aisle. Transeptal towers are of occasional occurrence, as at Bodmin St. Petrock (12) and Blisland in the same county, where they are attached to the north transept, and Ottery St. Mary in Devon, where they form a pair on either side of the building, following the arrangement at the mother-cathedral of Exeter. Whaplode in Lincolnshire and Clymping in Sussex have south transeptal towers, and at Melbury Bubb in Dorset the tower rises over a south porch projecting from an aisleless nave.

In certain cases, a belfry tower stands detached from the main building, an arrangement generally due to exigencies of the site, or to some defect in the ground. There are six such detached belfries in Cornwall, among them Telland and Gwennac, and other examples occur at East Dereham and West Walton (46) in Norfolk, Beccles in Suffolk, Sutton St. Mary in Lincolnshire (41), Elstow and Marston Moretaine in Bedfordshire, Ledbury and Pembridge (128), among others, in Herefordshire, Berkeley in Gloucestershire, Chittlehampton in Devon and Brookland in Kent.

Sometimes the western tower is engaged within the fabric, following an extension of the nave aisles. In such cases, three of its sides are supported on arches, those on the north and south opening into the aisles, as in the Lincolnshire churches of Grantham and Ewerby, and in some Cornish examples. At (e.g.) Keyworth in Nottinghamshire, Milford in Hampshire and elsewhere, the aisles were extended as lean-to additions to the tower walls, which were then pierced with low arches. Sometimes, again, the western tower stands out externally on piers, with archways north and south to a passage beneath it, as at Dedham in Essex, Wrotham in Kent and All Saints at Cambridge. This arrangement was adopted either to enable processions which could not leave consecrated ground to make the complete outdoor circuit of the church, or else, as at St. Mary's at Warwick, where a public highway encroached upon the site. The latter was also sometimes the cause of external vaulted passages beneath chancels, as at Hythe in Kent and Walpole St. Peter in Norfolk.

In the Eastern Counties, the towers of smaller village churches are often circular in plan and built of flint—a form possibly employed to avoid the expensive dressed quoin-stones necessary for square angles, which would have had to be brought from a distance (51). While octagonal upper lanterns are frequent (143), towers are occasionally built on this plan from the base up, as at Coxwold in Yorkshire, Stanwick in Northamptonshire and Standlake in Oxfordshire. At Uffing-ton in Berkshire (33) and Doulting in Somerset (44), among others, the octagonal upper stages rest upon square bases. Octagonal storeys built to form the transition to a spire are, of course, comparatively frequent, as at Wilby in Northampton-shire.

Finally, while the western tower is inseparably connected with the appearance of the English country church, it must be admitted that this position is open to criticism on aesthetic grounds, for it automatically precludes any effective design of the west front, generally so striking a feature of greater churches. At the same time, and more particularly during the later medieval centuries, tower-building grew to be one of the supreme achievements of the English masons, and their weathered productions are an integral feature of the landscape of the English Shires, whether half-hidden among trees or standing out in relief on upland ridges or against vast marshland skies.

THE PORCH (v. also p. 71)

The purpose of church porches was twofold—the utilitarian one of providing shelter and preserving the door from the weather; and for the performance of the earlier parts of the services of Baptism, Matrimony and Churching.

A pre-Conquest feature, possibly of monastic origin and rarely met with at later periods, was the rectangular west porch or narthex, usually with an opening on each face. Wherever this remains, it now forms the lower storey of a tower, as at Brixworth and at Monkwearmouth in Durham. At Bishopstone there is a Saxon south porch, and there were originally porches on both transept-arms of the Saxon chapel at Bradford-on-Avon.

Throughout the earlier Middle Ages there was usually, as has been seen, a single porch on the south side of the church. But though this tradition was an enduring one, the builders would not hesitate to infringe it where necessary—for instance, when the manor-house or the greater part of the village lay on the north side, as at Witney in Oxfordshire. Later, there was often a porch on both sides.

West porches are exceptional, but not nearly so rare as has sometimes been stated; Cley in Norfolk, Woodstock in Oxfordshire, King's Sutton in Northamptonshire, Yapton in Sussex, and Boxley and Otford in Kent may be cited as a few instances. The term "Galilee" is sometimes wrongly assigned to every west porch. The name arises from the frequent use made of this feature in the last stage of the Sunday procession; the celebrant, re-entering the church, was taken to symbolise Christ going before His disciples into Galilee after the Resurrection. It is probable, however, that in many smaller churches there was never a regular Sunday procession. Where it existed, the west porch was invariably the main congregational entrance, as the presence of holy-water stoups generally implies.

In a few churches, such as Weston-in-Gordano in Somerset, Caldicote in Monmouthshire and Wroxall in Warwickshire, there are the remains of small galleries inside the porches, probably used by the semi-chorus on Palm Sundays, which joined in special refrains when the procession made a station before entering the church. Upper chambers, often wrongly called parvises, were occasionally built over porches during the twelfth and thirteenth centuries; with the fourteenth they became fairly frequent, and with the fifteenth almost customary. Sometimes upper chambers were added to existing porches, as at Boston in Lincolnshire. The striking East-Anglian porches of the fourteenth and fifteenth centuries, with their beautiful stone and flint, or "flushwork," panelling, were almost invariably two-storeyed, as at Woolpit and Eye in Suffolk (144) and St. Nicholas' at King's Lynn (88).

The uses of these porch-chambers have been much discussed, but the theory that they were ever occupied by anchorites or hermits is discredited. In a few cases they are furnished with piscinas, as at Sall in Norfolk, showing that they contained altars and were used as occasional chapels. More often they contain fireplaces, especially the later ones, as at Westham in Kent and the beautiful structure at Northleach in Gloucestershire, where the smoke escaped through a cunningly devised vent in one of the bracketed pinnacles. Sometimes there are squints giving a fair general view of the church—not merely of the high altar—as at Mackworth in Derbyshire.

Perhaps the largest of these chambers are at Cirencester,

46 WEST WALTON, NORFOLK : The detached Thirteenth-century Bell-tower

47 CIRENCESTER, GLOUCESTERSHIRE : The Three-storeyed South Porch of the Fifteenth Century, with the rich Tower behind

where the magnificent south porch of three storeys (47) was used on its upper floors by the trade gilds of the town, afterwards serving for a time as the town hall. The north porch at Grantham was much enlarged during the fourteenth century, and its upper chamber fitted up as a chapel for the relics in the possession of the church. The south porch-chamber of the same building was clearly used by the night-watchman, who slept there; there is a small projecting window commanding a wide view of the interior. Other three-storeyed porches occur at Bodmin in Cornwall, Burford in Oxfordshire, and Bruton in Somerset, the latter resembling a small tower.

After the Reformation, porch-chambers were occasionally used as libraries; more often they served as stores for the parish armour. Where they were of a fair size they also sometimes became schoolrooms, as was the case at St. Sepulchre's in London, Colyton in Devonshire and Berkeley in Gloucestershire. Sunday school was held in the porch-rooms at Tottenham in Middlesex and Colby in Norfolk until as late as 1879, when a day school was still in existence in the porch at Malmesbury.

In addition to the types of western porches cited, there are cases of shallow porches or portals actually attached to western towers. The most beautiful example is the Early English one with twin entrances at Higham Ferrers in Northamptonshire; others can be seen at Raunds, Rushden, and Oundle in the same county. There are, it is believed, only two instances of a porch built over the priest's door in the chancel, namely at Trunch in Norfolk and Beccles in Suffolk.

THE VESTRY

On the north side of the chancel, or even occasionally at the east end, there is sometimes a rectangular addition, usually dating from the fourteenth century and differing from a chapel; this is the sacristy or vestry. In smaller churches, the priest sometimes robed in the space beneath the western tower or in some specially screened annex; nevertheless, definitely structural vestries were fairly common. These opened into the church by a door in the chancel wall, near the high altar, and where there was no external entrance probably also served as treasuries. Good examples occur at Worstead and Hingham in Norfolk, Islip in Northamptonshire and Burford in Oxfordshire; sometimes they contain a piscina, as at Hawton in Nottinghamshire, and occasionally they are of two storeys, as at Raunds in Northamptonshire and Chipping Norton in Oxfordshire. At Roos in Yorkshire, the upper storey is pro-

H

vided with a window looking into the chancel, probably for the night-watcher; more often, however, there is a squint commanding a view of the high altar. Now and again the upper' room contains a latrine, as at Warmington in Warwickshire.

Many vestries were added during the last century.

THE CRYPT

Crypts are rarely found in parish churches. Pre-Conquest examples survive at Repton, Brixworth, and Wing, and there are vaulted Norman ones at St. Mary-le-Bow in London, St. Peter's-in-the-East at Oxford, and under the chancel of the little Gloucestershire church of Duntisbourne Rous, where the ground falls away rather abruptly. There is a thirteenth-century vaulted crypt, also occasioned by a sloping site, under the east end of the chancel at Shillington in Bedfordshire, and fourteenth-century examples at Warrington in Lancashire and Madley in Herefordshire; but during the later Middle Ages this feature practically died out. With the fifteenth century, however, when great enlargements were made to parish churches, often encroaching on the graveyard, charnel- or bone-holes for the collection of the disturbed remains were sometimes formed under the new buildings, as at Newark in Nottinghamshire, Chipping Campden in Gloucestershire, and Witney in Oxfordshire.

* * *

The foregoing pages show something of the evolution of the parish-church plan in line with the development of ritual and the requirements of a changing social system. Before passing on to examine the structural design, it is good to remember the part played by the building in providing for the pleasures and relaxations of its parishioners, as well as for the cure of souls, calling all, in their various capacities, into its fellowship and service. Its immeasurable superiority at the close of the Middle Ages can be gauged by comparing the modest and severe little building raised by the Norman usurper of some Saxon manor with the fully developed structure of the fifteenth century, beautiful with colour, and leading the eye, by a gradual intensification of ornament, to the mystery of the inner sanctuary. It is not surprising that some five centuries were needed to attain this development, and it is sad to think how much that went to its beauty was swept away in the religious disorders of the next centuries.

48   GREAT BOOKHAM, SURREY: A Hamlet Church of the Home Counties

49 ST. CUTHBERT'S, WELLS, SOMERSET : A lofty Perpendicular
Reconstruction, with typical Somerset Roof (*vide* also fig. 38)

CHAPTER THREE

The Evolution of the Parish Church: the Structural Design

MEDIEVAL architecture was throughout its history in a state of varying transition, the character of the work changing repeatedly as one phase merged into the next. The builder was seldom content to let his craft stand still, but experimented with restless energy in the technique of construction and the forms of ornament.

The rate of advance was not always uniform, and contemporary work of the most diverse character can be seen in different parts of the country. Just as in human life it is difficult to define the exact limits of youth, manhood and middle age, so in the study of this architecture it is dangerous to resort too emphatically to an arbitrary classification by the "periods" dear to Victorian ecclesiologists. Its nomenclature has always been a thorny subject. The method here adopted follows that laid down in a companion volume on the Cathedrals, in which, broadly speaking, a classification by centuries was qualified by a reasonable use of Sharpe's and Rickman's labels, based chiefly on the styles of window tracery. For a fuller and reasoned discussion of this subject, however, the reader is recommended to an admirable section in Professor Lethaby's volume *Architecture* in the *Home University Library*.

While the architecture of the pre-Conquest and post-Conquest periods is generally here referred to as "Saxon" and "Norman" respectively, it should be emphasised that these were both offshoots of the same Romanesque stem that flourished grandly in Western Europe for over three centuries. Again, the term Transitional is used in a broad sense to designate the period of change towards the close of the twelfth century from the massive forms of Romanesque to the constructional subtleties of Gothic, embracing a wide field of experiment and adaptation. With the thirteenth century appears the first distinctive English variant of early Gothic, labelled alternatively "Early English" and "Lancet" by schools of nineteenth-century opinion, culminating towards the close of the century, with the advent of window tracery in the "Geometrical" phase, in which as considerable an authority as Professor Prior has somewhat surprisingly seen the peak of English medieval achievement. With the opening years of the fourteenth century came a relaxation of these geometric patterns into a variety of sinuous "flowing" or "Curvilinear" forms, with a brief outburst of rather facile naturalistic ornament, that marks the so-called "Decorated" phase, coincident with the English Age of Chivalry. After 1350, the cleavage in tradition wrought by the Black Death gave admission to a new and original method of surface decoration, relying for its effects on the application of rectilinear transomed tracery and light stone panelling, with a general enlargement of windows, for which the term "Perpendicular" has generally come to be accepted. This new manner, the development of which, with its rich ancillary craftsmanship, is discussed later in the chapter, constituted the most considerable contribution of the English builders to medieval architecture, and is without parallel at its period in other countries. Enduring for two clear centuries and well into a third, it is the most distinctive vernacular style in the long history of English building.

CIRCA 600 TO 1066

Such, very briefly, is an outline of the great process of development in which the parish church played a contributory part, a process that begins some centuries before the Norman Conquest. The main types of churches at this earliest period have already been analysed. As regards their construction, there is little doubt that most of them were built of wood, following an old timber tradition common to Northern Europe. Inevitably, from the nature of the material, these buildings have nearly all vanished or been replaced, but a unique example survives, much restored, at Greenstead-by-Ongar in Essex (52), where the small rectangular nave, dating from the opening years of the eleventh century, and probably the very chapel built to receive the body of St. Edmund on its last journey from London to St. Edmundsbury in 1013, is built palisade-fashion of upright split oak-trunks smoothed with the adze on their flat faces. The style and technique of this building were probably fairly general throughout England for most of the pre-Conquest period, when, whatever the structural limitations, there was certainly never a shortage of building timber.

In this connection, a little-noticed passage in the Ramsey Pontifical of the close of the eleventh century is significant. This envisages the possibility of a bishop being called upon to consecrate a timber church by providing that, if the building was of wood (*si vero lignea fuerat*), the antiphon *Vidit Jacob scalam* was to take the place of *Lapides preciosi*.

Again, owing to the difficulties of quarrying and transporting stone, a considerable use was made, especially in stoneless districts such as East Anglia, of the Roman bricks that were still to be found in large quantities about the country in the decaying monuments of the old Imperial colonisers. There are distinctive examples of their use in the arches of the arcade at Brixworth and the triangular-headed windows in the church of the Holy Trinity at Colchester, among others. Nevertheless, as Romanesque influence asserted itself, stone was naturally the most favoured material, notably the fine oolitic limestone of Barnack in Northamptonshire, though instances persisted of the use of Roman squared or sculptured stones in Saxon fabrics, as at Escomb in County Durham.

An examination of this little building of the seventh century probably provides as graphic an idea of the appearance of the typical Saxon stone church as is possible from surviving examples. Its marked characteristic is its great height in relation to its ground dimensions, and the insignificant size of its chancel, which opens out of the nave by little more than a tall arch-doorway (50). These traits are also seen in the Saxon chapel at Bradford-on-Avon in Wiltshire (26) and the church at Wareham in Dorset. Where there is a western tower, a semicircular arch of rough masonry often gives access to it from the nave, as at Deerhurst in Gloucestershire, or forms an exterior west door, as at Earl's Barton in Northamptonshire.

A review of the structural features of Saxon building shows that the walls were as a rule well constructed, but thinner than the Norman, varying in depth from 2 to $3\frac{1}{2}$ feet. Plaster originally covered most of the walling, inside and out, but Saxon chevron tooling, as opposed to the diagonal stroke of the Norman axe, often appears on the larger masonry, as on the interior of the tower at St. Benet's at Cambridge and the jambstones of the windows at Wansford in Northamptonshire. The treatment of the outer angles of the buildings was twofold. In the one case, the quoin-stones were arranged in the famous "long and short" manner, in which upright squared stones from 2 to 4 feet in height were alternated with flat slabs projecting beyond the angles and gripping into the wall, as at Earl's Barton. Sometimes also the horizontal stone was cut back to the width of the upright quoin. In the other case, large squares of stone were massed irregularly one above the other, as at St. Mildred's at Canterbury, Stow in Lincolnshire, Escomb, and St. Peter-on-the-Walls in Essex.

The pilaster-strip was another characteristic feature, as at Breamore, Barton-on-Humber, Stanton Lacy in Shropshire, and in the towers of Earl's Barton (82) and Sompting.

These strips consist of flat upright stone battens, varying in width from 5 to 13 inches, but projecting only an inch or two from the walls. They are structurally too slight to be regarded as anything but ornamental, and the theory of Strzygowski and others that they were an adaptation in stone of earlier timber-frame methods, though attractive, seems hardly tenable.

The double-splayed window was a feature of frequent occurrence, the outer splay being generally the slighter. Good examples occur at Boarhunt, Barton-on-Humber, Diddlebury in Shropshire, and Wareham. Equally characteristic were the two-light openings of belfry windows. Each half of the aperture was surmounted by a small round arch, both generally cut out of the same stone; and between them was a stone prop or shaft, usually of a baluster form, as though turned on a lathe. Triple and multiple openings of this kind are sometimes found, as, internally, at Brixworth (25), and at Earl's Barton (82). Triangular-headed openings were also characteristic, with two inclined slabs forming the sides of the triangle, as at Barnack and Deerhurst.

Only brief mention can be made of the fragmentary examples of carving and ornament that have survived from pre-Conquest times. That the earlier Saxon craftsmen could produce figure-sculpture of strength and severe dignity is apparent from so fine a work as the seventh-century Bewcastle Cross in Cumberland, while scraps of their incised stonework, with its animal ornament and interlacements, can be seen in various parish churches, including Fletton in Huntingdonshire and Breedon in Leicestershire—in both of which fragments of figure-carving also remain. The work of the earlier eleventh century is represented in a group of tympana and dignified sculptured wall-roods, as at Romsey in Hampshire and Langford in Oxfordshire, while a pair of carved slabs, now built into the wall of the south quire aisle of Chichester Cathedral, show the heights to which the sculpture of the immediate pre-Conquest period could occasionally rise.

CIRCA 1066 TO 1180

The architecture of Saxon England, though abounding in works of individual interest, was haphazard and unorganised in its manifestations. As in every other branch of production, the Norman infusion brought order and energy into the science of building, substituting for individualism and experiment a considered and methodical style which the building enthusiasm of the twelfth century was to propagate solidly

51 BESSINGHAM, NORFOLK : An early Flint
Round Tower

50 ESCOMB, COUNTY DURHAM:
The Saxon Chancel

52 GREENSTEAD-JUXTA-ONGAR, ESSEX, showing the archaic
Timber Nave

53 ST. PETER'S, NORTHAMPTON: The rich Norman Nave Arcade

and impressively throughout the country. The forms of the new churches have been set forth in the previous chapter; it now remains to give some account of their structural design, their appearance, and their ornament.

The chief characteristic of the earlier Norman churches is their massiveness of masonry, the walls being often some 4 feet thick, built with flat pilaster-like buttresses of slight projection which served no more than an ornamental purpose in providing relief and defining the bays of an elevation. As a general rule, the masonry was of small-stone type, with wide jointing in the earlier examples. Sometimes, however, churches were entirely built of rubble faced with squared ashlar stones, which, when carelessly put together, rendered them liable to serious later disintegration. The type known as herring-bone occurs in much earlier Norman rubble walling, as also in pre-Conquest and even Roman buildings. Where rubble was used, the quoins and facings were at first chiefly of Caen freestone imported from Normandy, but later Barnack stone was much employed, with the various magnesian limestones of the North. With the twelfth century, the masonry joints also became much finer.

In the rare earlier buildings, the arches were simply molded, the capitals of the plainest cushion type, and the windows, in smaller churches at least, often little more than slits in the deep walls. But with the twelfth century came an outburst of fresh ornament, expressing itself not only in the carving of tympana, capitals, shafts and other features, but in a rich variety of decorative moldings. Of these, the earliest was the chevron or zigzag, soon to be followed, especially on doorways, by the characteristic beak-head motive, of which the south door at Kilpeck (55) is so rich an example. Other types were the cable, billet, lozenge, pellet, studd, chain, cone, scallop, and star, too numerous for analysis, but all boldly effective in their application.

The later doorways were frequently recessed in successive planes known as orders, each with its shaft and capital, often heavily carved. The semicircular stones, or tympana, with which the heads of their arches were filled were either carved with geometric ornament, as in the little church of Kilpeck in Herefordshire, or with sculpture in low relief, as at Aston Eyre in Shropshire, combining hieratic figures, birds, and animals with interlacements reminiscent of Celtic and Scandinavian art. The windows, insignificant at first, grew larger in size, now often incorporating shafts with capitals inside and out, as at Stow in Lincolnshire. The circular

"wheel" window, with radiating "spokes," is also characteristic, as at Barfreston in Kent, but this feature was on the
whole confined to larger churches. The arches of the arcades,
and more particularly the chancel arches, were treated with
bold incisive moldings. Good examples can be seen in
most counties, but particular mention might be made of the
chancel arches at Wakerley in Northamptonshire, Walsoken
in Norfolk, Winchfield in Hampshire, and Kilpeck, which are
among the finest.

Capitals were largely of two well-defined types, the "cushion"
(which probably originated in this country) and the "volute,"
and covered a wide range from the simple to the ornate.
The cushion type is of wide distribution, and the volute is
also quite frequent, as, for instance, at St. Peter's at Northampton (53) and St. Woolos' at Newport in Monmouthshire (105).
In parish churches piers were usually of simple octagonal or
cylindrical form, occasionally banded or grooved in patterns;
the plainer examples were merely painted with diapers.
A favourite feature, of structural as well as ornamental importance in tying together and strengthening rubble walling,
was the stone wall-arcade, used both inside and out, of plain
or interlaced arches of varying projection, often richly carved.
String-courses, cornices, and corbel-tables received a similar
ornamental treatment.

So many Norman churches have survived all over the
country that it is hard to make a choice of examples, but,
beyond those cited, mention should certainly be made of the
little Heath Chapel above Corve Dale in Shropshire (27),
lying simple and untouched in secluded country, the slightly
larger church of similar type at Adel in Yorkshire, the still
small but richly ornamented churches of Iffley in Oxfordshire
and Barfreston in Kent, and the large and stately fabrics of
Hemel Hempstead, St. Peter's at Northampton (53) and
Melbourne in Derbyshire (56). Impressive as their interiors
are to-day, they can only give a half-hearted impression of
their original beauty when finished with smooth plaster and
deep colour. The polychromatic schemes are largely lost to us,
but it is often possible to recapture something of their character
from the faded traces of old colouring that still cling to many
an arch-mold and pillar in churches about the country.

CIRCA 1140 TO 1170

The processes of the change to Gothic are puzzling, and
the use of the label Transitional is certainly to be deplored

54　ELKSTONE, GLOUCESTERSHIRE : The Vaulted Norman Chancel

55　KILPECK, HEREFORDSHIRE : Norman Grotesques around the
South Doorway

56 MELBOURNE, DERBYSHIRE: The Norman Nave, looking East

57 CASTLE HEDINGHAM, ESSEX: The Late-Norman Nave Arcade

if it implies the existence of any separate intermediate style following after the Romanesque. The period generally was one of wavering development quickened by spasms of energetic experiment. Features typical of early Gothic make their appearance in otherwise thoroughly Romanesque fabrics, and, conversely, Romanesque elements, such as the cushion capital and round arch, are found persisting in churches that reflect structurally the new ideas of Gothic.

Among the parish churches, the effects of this movement are represented in a rather fragmentary way. To understand something of the forces at work it is essential to turn to the larger buildings, where such precocious and intensely interesting experiments as were carried out by twelfth-century builders in the western bays of the Worcester nave and the original fabric of Ripon Minster go to refute the old suggestion that Gothic was imported ready-made into this country from the Île de France when William of Sens was summoned to Canterbury to superintend the building of the new quire.

One of the strongest forces in the Transitional flux was probably the austere tradition of Cistercian building, with its absence of ornament and advanced moldings, as can be seen in the ruins of the great Northern abbeys of the later twelfth century—Fountains, Kirkstall, and Furness. This influence must have had its reaction on parish church design, but the lapse of seven and a half centuries, with their record of rebuilding, redecorating and patching, has made the scent faint, and the majority of investigators have turned their noses from the wind. It is of interest, however, that so positive and voluminous an authority as Professor Pijoan has suggested that the first experiments in ogival building belonged to the smaller rather than the greater churches.

Among churches reflecting these tendencies, mention must be made of the beautiful interior at Castle Hedingham in Essex (57), with its graceful arcade of definite Early English suggestion in the capitals. A more composite and less successful blending of the two elements occurs at Whitechurch Canonicorum in Dorset, and there is a group in the Nene Valley of Northamptonshire that can show many interesting vagaries, including Warmington, where cushion capitals support pointed arches, Polebrook, and Deeping St. James, where the round arches of the nave arcade have full-formed Gothic moldings. Pointed Norman chancel arches occur in several twelfth-century churches, such as Walsoken in Norfolk and Bredon in Worcestershire, while some thirteenth-century arcades, as that of St. Mary's at

I

Shrewsbury, have round-headed arches and very simple moldings. Such combinations were almost endless, and their best pictorial catalogue is still Sharpe's great unfinished work on *The Ornamentation of the Transitional Period in British Architecture*, though again the majority of examples illustrated are from greater churches.

CIRCA 1170 TO 1260

It was not until the second decade of the thirteenth century that a consistent Gothic began to be applied to parish churches, where, since vaulting was seldom used, the transformation, at least structurally, was not destined to be so radical as in larger fabrics. Nevertheless, the revolution in technique was far-reaching. The old system of static construction, in which the outward thrust of a vault or roof was counteracted by the continuous abutment of massive walls, now began to be replaced by one that can only be described as dynamic, in that each separate thrust was met by a counterthrust, the equilibrium being so delicate that the failure of an element might easily involve the collapse of the whole. Throughout all the phases of Gothic, the builders strove consistently towards an increased space and height and lighter construction, involving a steady reduction in the thickness of the wall masonry as it was pierced by larger areas of window. In the greater churches, the thrust of the vault was concentrated at fixed points along the walls, where it was met by exterior buttressing, either solid from the ground or in the form of free-standing arch-segments, called flying-buttresses. This system of building with light buttressed walls was naturally enough followed in parish churches, even though a timber roof was substituted for a stone vault.

The pointed arch, which became so constant a feature of the Gothic style, was a logical result of the solution of problems in ribbed vaulting, though it was never the constructional essential that some earlier scholars have considered it to be, and Gothic buildings might (and occasionally did) retain the rounded form. The suggestions of its derivation from intersecting semicircular arches, or from the East, through the agency of the Crusades, are now largely discredited.

The first phase of Gothic in this country, known for almost a hundred years as Early English, though its serious simplicity dignifies churches in most districts, is best judged in its purity in a group of greater buildings that includes the cathedrals of Salisbury, Lincoln, and Wells. Nevertheless, some beautiful

58 STONE, KENT : A richly-carved Interior of the Thirteenth Century

59 WEST WALTON, NORFOLK: Thirteenth Century

60 THAXTED, ESSEX: Fourteenth Century

A Century of Evolution in English Gothic

work of the thirteenth century exists in parish churches, though only a handful, such as Skelton in Yorkshire, War-mington in Northamptonshire, West Walton in Norfolk (59), Uffington in Berkshire (33), Potterne in Wiltshire and Etton in Northamptonshire, still give any consistent impression of the parochial application of the style at this period. The interiors of these churches are for the most part simple and reserved; their lancet windows admit comparatively little light (24), and the general impression is one of dignity and severity rather than the bright serenity of the later centuries.

The main characteristics of the style are too familiar to need much recapitulation. The windows were tall and narrow, of simple lancet type, and, where not placed singly, were arranged in groups of three, five, or even seven, as in the trio at Witney (24), the Five Sisters of Bosham in Sussex, and the sevenfold east window at Ockham in Surrey. Some-times the groups were ar-ranged within larger containing arches, as at Etton. The piers, while still generally plainly octagonal or cylindrical, were occasionally formed of slender free-standing shafts grouped around a central member, as at Eaton Bray in Bedfordshire and West Walton in Norfolk.

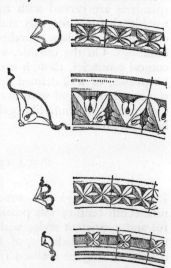

"DOG-TOOTH" OR "NAIL-HEAD" ORNAMENT AND ITS APPLICATION

The capitals, in parish churches at least, were for the most part molded, as at Great Brington in Northamptonshire (61), but examples are occasionally found worked with the new type of stiff-leaf foliage, deeply undercut and usually very effective, as may be seen at Eaton Bray, West Walton (64) and Stone in Kent (58), a wonderful repository of thirteenth-century carving. The bases of the piers have a certain affinity with those of classic architecture, and generally incorporate the characteristic hollow between rolls known as the "water-holding molding."

The pointed arches were also cut with moldings, ranging from plain chamfers to deep and intricate profiles of many members, etched with sharp lines of shadow and often enriched with one or more rows of the carved pyramidal "nail-head" or "dog-tooth" ornament so popular at this phase. The same motive was much applied to corbel-tables, cornices, and doorways, and was used with striking effect for the enrichment of recessed orders, as in the fine west doorway at Warmington in Northamptonshire and the south doorways of Mumby in Lincolnshire and Skelton in Yorkshire. Arcading was employed as a decorative feature on walls and towers, either simple or interlaced, as at St. Mary's at Stamford, Raunds in Northamptonshire, and Stone in Kent, where the spandrels are carved with foliage; but the use of Purbeck marble shafting for this and other features, so popular in cathedral and abbey churches, is seldom found in parochial buildings. On the outside, a certain use was made of plain conical pinnacles, though mainly in larger churches, and the buttresses, of well-defined projection, were built in receding stages, often scored with horizontal lines at the courses and terminating in knife-like gablets, as at Higham Ferrers in Northamptonshire.

CIRCA 1260 TO 1300

Such, briefly, were the broad characteristics of "Early English." Though the reverential enthusiasm of the later nineteenth century was possibly exaggerated, it was a forceful and consistent style, with all the vigour, besides something of the coltishness, of adolescence; for an adolescence it was, as may be realised from so incongruous an essay in front design as occurs, among other instances, at Wyck Rissington in the Cotswolds. The thirteenth century marked the peak of episcopal ambition and dignity in England, and much of this was reflected in the adornment of the churches, the culmination being reached during the third quarter in works of the calibre of the Ely Presbytery and the Lincoln Angel Choir. The burgeoning spread through every department of building, and by *circa* 1260 can be definitely observed in the design of parish churches.

As ever in Gothic, the newest developments were written in the windows. About half-way through the century the lancet began to lose its familiar outline and grow broader, and the earliest "plate-tracery" was evolved by piercing the solid masonry between a pair of windows and their containing dripstone with circles, trefoils, quatrefoils, and other patterns. At Brownsover in Warwickshire, the space over twin lancets was cut with a lozenge-shaped opening; at Kilworth in

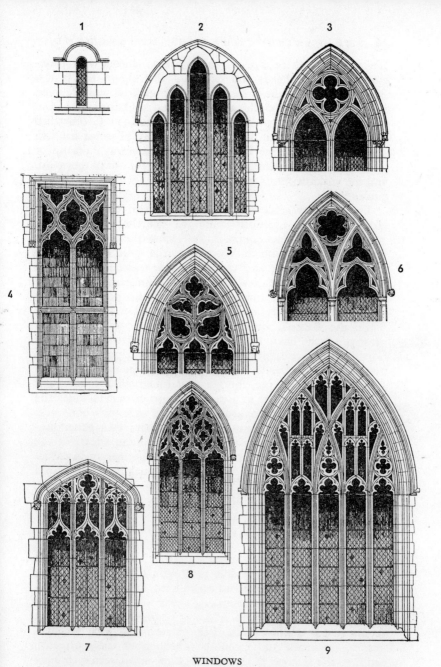

WINDOWS

1. Norman (Barfreston, Kent); 2. Early English (Oundle, Northants); 3. Geometrical (West Walton, Norfolk); 4. Reticulated (Northborough, Northants); 5. Curvilinear (Frampton, Lincs); 6. Geometrical-Curvilinear (Ely Chapel, London); 7. Perpendicular (Cherry Hinton, Cambs); 8. Curvilinear-Perpendicular (Houghton-le-Dale, Norfolk); 9. Perpendicular (Wawn, Yorkshire)

Leicestershire there is a range of paired lancets with plate-tracery at their heads and detached shafting in the jambs. Soon the space in the head of a double window was occupied by a plainly cusped circle, as at St. Giles' at Oxford, and from thence it was a short step to the full-formed Geometrical tracery that has given its name to an entire phase of English design. In this, for the first time, the tracery was built up of a framework of stone mullions rather than cut out of the solid, and the window-heads patterned with arrangements of cusped circles (66).

The maturity achieved at this phase was reflected in enlargements and additions made to churches all over the country. In the Northamptonshire group alone there are the beautiful south porch of Woodford, the spire of Crick, the tower of Harleston, and the north aisle and Lady Chapel of Higham Ferrers. The great church of St. Wulfram at Grantham is one of the most impressive works of this period, though the fabric incorporates much of later date. Here, in about 1280, while the Lincoln builders nearby were completing their presbytery, the nave was extended two bays to the west, the north aisle practically completed, and the magnificent tower begun. Temple Balsall Chapel in Warwickshire is another almost perfect example, though on a much smaller scale, and Oxfordshire can show an interesting group that includes the chancel of Hampton Poyle and the south aisle of Woodstock. This list could be continued much further; as a generalisation, churches throughout the country felt the effects of the new fashion in enlargements, elaboration or merely in casual window insertions, of which Crawley in Buckinghamshire and Rickinghall Inferior in Suffolk, among countless others, furnish very typical examples.

CIRCA 1300 TO 1350

The term "Decorated," used since the days of John Britton to designate the next phase, is a little misleading in that, though greater churches now achieved an ornamental exuberance previously unsurpassed, those of country districts often remained modest in size and plain in design, without sculpture and lacking much of the thirteenth-century incisiveness of ornament and molding. Throughout the fourteenth century, the quality of the architectural detail seems to have varied more than at any other period. At its best it is magnificent, but some village churches can show a masoncraft as poor as anything in English building.

61 GREAT BRINGTON, NORTHAMPTONSHIRE : The late Thirteenth-
century Arcade, with moulded Capitals and hollow-sided Piers

62 WEST COUNTRY PERPENDICULAR : Wolborough, Devon

63 DECORATED : Patrington, Yorkshire

64 EARLY ENGLISH : West Walton, Norfolk

ENGLISH GOTHIC CAPITALS

But as a whole the period was one of brisk architectural progress and experiment in vaulting, window tracery and construction generally. Hitherto France had been supreme as the source of new ideas; now England was largely isolated from the Continent, self-dependent, and free of its domination. Up to the catastrophe of the Black Death of 1350 the spirit of the century was light-hearted, graceful, chivalrous; the architecture that was its reflection was to form the germ of the more extreme and less subtle French *Flamboyant* of the next century, after English taste had evolved in its turn the rich sobriety of Perpendicular.

From about 1300 onwards, one steadfast tendency is apparent in English building: the growth of the conception of the church as a stone framework for its carved features and painted windows. Everywhere windows grew in size, the

"BALLFLOWER" ORNAMENT AND ITS APPLICATION

conventional Geometrical tracery now giving way to a wide range of graceful experiment in flowing and leaping patterns (68) that provide one of the most attractive achievements of later medieval design. These Curvilinear forms must have resulted in part from the cult of the ogee arch, which became so distinctive a structural fashion of the first half of the century, and persisted well into the second.

The development of carving was revolutionary. In its figure-sculpture for tombs and other features the period was supreme, while ornament achieved a brief new luxuriance of form and application in leaf and plant carving—though after 1320 plainly molded capitals were generally employed. Gables and pinnacles were encrusted with carved crockets, and the "ballflower" ornament appeared in its myriads to replace the thirteenth-century dog-tooth in the enrichment, not only of pinnacles and spires, but of moldings, arches and windows (67), as in the north aisles at Badgeworth in Gloucestershire and St. Catherine's Chapel at Ledbury in Herefordshire. Churches were now, where funds and talent were available, clothed with an extraordinary elegance of carving, an elegance that remains fresh and unspoilt to-day in such beautiful Decorated essays as Heckington in Lincolnshire (121) and Patrington in Yorkshire (45), with their wealth of crocketed pinnacles, pierced parapets, and graceful little tabernacles for a vanished figure-sculpture.

These two are supremely representative among parish churches of the earlier fourteenth century at its richest. Less elaborate work, but none the less effective, is to be found at Hawton in Nottinghamshire, Nantwich in Cheshire, Crick and Ringstead in Northamptonshire, Yaxley in Huntingdonshire, Hedon and Howden in Yorkshire, Norbury in Derbyshire, and the portion of Cley in Norfolk left unfinished at the time of the Black Death. One of the most interesting groups occurs among the Fenlands of Lincolnshire, where in such churches as Holbeach, Swaton, Billingborough and the splendid St. Botolph's at Boston (4), the Curvilinear fashion can be studied at the height of its exuberance. Kegworth in Leicestershire and Pembridge in Herefordshire may be instanced as examples of plainer rebuilding.

Many other churches were enlarged or refenestrated, and, while it would be difficult to make a full survey of the new tracery patterns, it should be remembered that the Geometrical tradition died hard, and forms such as the cusped wheel and quatrefoil were at first often retained in otherwise Curvilinear designs, as can be seen at Hawkhurst in Kent, St. Catherine's Chapel at Ledbury, Leominster (67) and the great west window at Snettisham in Norfolk. In other churches, a plainer type of reticulated tracery was sometimes standardised, as at Hoby in Leicestershire and the east end of Higham Ferrers; and occasionally the openings were flat- or segmental-headed, as at Tideswell in Derbyshire and Over in Cambridgeshire respectively.

Piers were now generally simpler in form, ranging from plain octagons to the four-membered type so characteristic of the period, dispensing with the free-standing shaft and often with a plain fillet on the outer edges of the members. The arches were now more simply molded, a characteristic profile being the ogee, or wave, while sometimes moldings were continuous through pier and arch, without a capital. Carved capitals were the exception rather than the rule in parish churches, though fine examples can be cited, as at Finedon in Northamptonshire and at Patrington (63). But there was compensation in the ornamental beauty of other fittings and features, such as tombs, fonts, tabernacles, and particularly sedilia and Easter Sepulchres, of which the examples at Hawton and

65   PATRINGTON, YORKSHIRE : An almost perfect Interior of the Fourteenth Century (*vide* also figs. 45 and 63)

66 GEOMETRICAL : Grantham

67 GEOMETRICAL : Leominster, with Ballflower Encrustation

68 CURVILINEAR : St. Mary's, Beverley

69 EARLY PERPENDICULAR : Edington, Wiltshire

ENGLISH GOTHIC WINDOW TRACERY

NAVE ARCADES

1. Norman (Deeping St. James, Lincs); 2. Transitional (Woodford, Northants);
3. Early English (Higham Ferrers, Northants); 4. Decorated (Finedon,
Northants); 5. Perpendicular (Whiston, Northants); 6. Perpendicular
(Fotheringay, Northants).

K

Heckington stand supreme, with their foliage and delicate figuring. Here it must be remembered, however, that from about 1300 on, the majority of such works were executed in the great craft shops now established in important centres such as London for the working of Caen and Reigate stone, Exeter for Beer stone, Gloucester for Cheltenham stone, Norwich for clunch, and so on, the features being delivered piecemeal and assembled on the spot, much as they would be to-day.

CIRCA 1350 TO 1535

In the spring of its achievement, the work of the fourteenth century was cut short by the epidemic of the Black Death of 1348–49, which in two years carried off a third of the population of England and paralysed for several more all architectural activity. Its interruption to work in progress is apparent all over the country, and in parish churches this was generally followed by a change in plan and style, as may be well seen in the great churches of Newark, Great Yarmouth, and Cley-on-Sea. It was during this period of interruption that the so-called Perpendicular manner gained its first sure footing in English church design.

It was in *circa* 1340 that the Gloucester monks, with the offerings brought to the shrine of the canonised Edward II, decided on the reconstruction of the eastern limb of their church as a splendid mortuary chapel to the profitable saint. To carry out this work, they employed the advanced and original masons of the so-called Severn school, whose experiments in a new technique of openwork construction must already have attracted notice in their vaulting of the Bristol Abbey quire. But it was at Gloucester that their ideas took most vital form. The new quire was one of the most striking examples of pure originality in the history of Western building. Here a new style was not evolved patiently over a period of years, but arrived at, as it were, overnight.

It was significant that the work was not a thoroughgoing rebuilding but a recasing of the old Romanesque core with a scaffolding of light masonry, designed to give the maximum of effect with the minimum of labour and expense. It was first and foremost a style of surface decoration achieved by rectilinear cusped panelling, the framework of which was continued in the horizontal transoms and slender vertical mullions of the windows of many lights. By such means, the great quire was transformed into a single-storeyed design of splendid

70 THE GREENWAY CHAPEL, TIVERTON, DEVON: An unusual
example of flamboyance in Perpendicular Masoncraft

71 CURRY RIVEL, SOMERSET: The developed Perpendicular
technique of the West Country

72 LAVENHAM, SUFFOLK: An East Anglian Achievement of *circa* 1500

spaciousness and height, rising in the clerestory to a lantern of tall windows and crowned with a lierne vault of endless elaboration. From such a result, it would be a short step to the conception of the church as a broad aisleless hall, to all intents and purposes walled with panelled glass, to which the later development of fan-vaulting provided an appropriate crowning feature. Buildings such as the Chapels of St. George at Windsor and King's College at Cambridge merely carried the revolution of Gloucester to its logical ends.

Compared with the subtleties of Curvilinear design, the new manner was immeasurably simpler in its setting out and rendering. With the scarcity of skilled labour that followed the Pestilence, when masons had regularly to be empressed for the Royal Works, it must have been hailed as a godsend by the many scratch teams of raw or half-trained workmen who were now called upon to wrestle with the quite considerable problems of church building and extension. Such causes were undoubtedly instrumental in the almost universal adoption of Perpendicular towards the close of the century, and account for the paucity of transitional examples, though the once priory church of Edington in Wiltshire (*circa* 1360) is an interesting study. It was markedly in the Eastern Counties, however, that the builders clung with most affection to their curving patterns, and here many hybrid tracery experiments are on record, as at Soham in Cambridgeshire.

If, with the adoption of Perpendicular, the technique of masoncraft grew more stereotyped, there was compensation in the revival of woodworking during the second half of the fourteenth century, when the carpenter, shaking himself free of masonic convention, produced an outburst of craftsmanship in stalls, screens, benches, roofs and the like, which ranks among the real splendours of English art. Now the wheel had swung, and the fifteenth-century mason was not unwilling to follow the carpenter's lead or to borrow from his designs. Similarly, if ironwork suffered a decline, the nature of the new style brought about a fine activity in glass-painting, and the silvery hues of the fifteenth century rank among the loveliest productions of this damaged and almost obliterated art.

Perpendicular, then, had firmly established its hold by the close of the fourteenth century. So far as church building was concerned, it was to flourish without interruption until the Reformation (*circa* 1535), when activity on the old scale abruptly ceased. While occasional work of an ecclesiastical nature was carried on after the breach, its productions thenceforward were largely domestic and collegiate, in which spheres, in spite of an accretion of immature Renaissance detail, the style of buildings continued medieval in feeling until well into the seventeenth century.

The chief decorative innovation of the new style was, as has been seen, its system of surface treatment with cusped stone panelling. This, though seldom employed among the parish churches for large areas of walling, was much used in chantry chapels and tombs, on buttresses, and in the jambs and soffits of arches and doorways, as at St. Lawrence's at Evesham and Yelverton in Northamptonshire. The recti-linear framing of doorways became almost universal, the triangular spandrels formed being usually filled with cusped circles and panelled or heraldic ornament, as at Copdock in Suffolk; and in later churches, a similar treatment was sometimes applied with rich effect to the spandrels of the arcade, as at Lavenham (35), Whiston in Northamptonshire and St. Mary's at Beverley. As the style advanced, the arches themselves became increasingly of the depressed four-centred type, in doors, windows and even occasionally arcades, as at Whiston in Northamptonshire (p. 62); while innumerable later windows were square-headed. The tracery largely followed the forms of the panelling, with cusping, horizontal transoms and vertical mullions, now carried straight into the heads of the windows instead of diverging as soon as the springing of the arches was reached—an arrangement particularly suitable to the glass-painter. The patterning of such window-heads was by no means as stereotyped as some critics have main-tained; a review of the best work shows a wide range of often excellent designs, with some well-defined local types, par-ticularly in the South-West; and some of the more ambitious windows are superb, as, almost at random, at Colyton in Devon, the east end of St. Margaret's at Lowestoft, the west end of St. Nicholas' at King's Lynn and the east window at Patrington (45, 65).

A plain octagonal pillar continued in use throughout the style, but with considerable variations of shallow concave moldings and fillets. In composite piers, which were often built on a roughly lozenge-shaped plan with attached shafting at the four corners, the arch-molds were frequently con-tinuous, with neat independent capitals on the shafts only, as at St. Margaret's at Lowestoft and St. Lawrence's at Ludlow. These capitals generally took the form of plain engaged octagons, sometimes enriched with compact foliage, as at Tickhill in Yorkshire, or occasionally with battlementing or figure-sculpture of heraldic type, such as the angels holding

74 LONG MELFORD, SUFFOLK : The
Fifteenth-century Nave

73 DEEPING ST. JAMES, LINCOLNSHIRE :
The Transitional Arcade

75 ST. PETER MANCROFT, NORWICH: A great Town Church,
completed in 1455

76 ASHBURTON, DEVON: A typical Tower of this County,
with mid-side Stair-turret

77 ST. STEPHEN'S, WALBROOK, LONDON: A Church Interior
by Sir Christopher Wren (1676-8)

shields at St. Petrock's at Exeter. A wide range of carved motives and devices was employed for cornices, cresting, label-heads and other features in wood and stone, including the four-leaf flower, the vine-leaf, heraldic shields, beasts and badges, personal rebuses, emblems of the saints, and, latterly, the Tudor rose and portcullis.

On the outside, even the largest churches built at this period are generally lighter and more graceful than their predecessors. Their fine towers are described in the next chapter; their walls were pierced with majestic areas of window, now practically continuous in the clerestory. Their low-pitched roofs were masked with parapets and battlements, and there was a heraldic stateliness of pinnacle and buttress. On the inside, if to their less friendly critics the effect is sometimes cold and bare, it must be remembered that they are now only judging the stone framework of a rich and magnificent *ensemble*, to which the crafts of the glass-painter and carver supplied the culminating ingredients of colour and subtle detail. Even bleached and stripped of their fittings as they are to-day, there can be few, however, who would deny the fine spaciousness and dignity of great churches such as St. Peter Mancroft at Norwich (75), St. Lawrence's at Ludlow, Saffron Walden in Essex (39), Walpole St. Peter (17) and Terrington St. Clement (29, 37) in Norfolk, and Chipping Campden and Cirencester (47) in Gloucestershire; the effectiveness of lesser buildings such as Bruton in Somerset, Fairford (11) in Gloucestershire and Whiston in Northamptonshire; or the individual exuberance of such examples as the almost totally carved granite church of Launceston in Cornwall and the little Greenway Chapel at Tiverton in Devon (70).

CIRCA 1535 TO 1660

There was probably less church building and maintenance carried out during the reign of Elizabeth than in any other half-century within the scope of this survey. With a few exceptions, such as the little brick church of Woodham Walter in Essex, with its timber bellcote and crow-stepped Tudor gables, built by Elizabeth's Earl of Essex in 1562–63, Watton in Yorkshire, with its square-headed windows, dating from *circa* 1550, and the virtual reconstruction of Hanley in Worcestershire, the Elizabethan contribution to church art was negligible, mostly confined to fittings and tombs. For the first half of the seventeenth century conditions were much the same, St. John's at Leeds being the only considerable production—a curious design with twin naves and a magnificent array of contemporary fittings. A number of older churches, however, were rebuilt, as Fulmer (1610) and Bletchley (1637) in Buckinghamshire, Stowe-Nine-Churches (1620), and Passenham (1626) in Northamptonshire, Carrington (1648) in Derbyshire, Staunton Harold (1653) in Leicestershire, and a group in Kent that includes St. Nicholas' at Rochester (1620), Groombridge (1621) and Charlton (1640). George Herbert reconstructed the ruinous church of Leighton Bromswold in Huntingdonshire about 1634, with a range of woodwork fittings.

These buildings were plain and solid in design, their detail reflecting the Renaissance influence and their most decorative features being generally their hammer-beam roofs (*v.* p. 79), their screens and their pulpits, as at Croscombe in Somerset (20) and the refurnished Cistercian church of Abbey Dore in Herefordshire. Hampshire can show some effective brick towers, including Odiham (1647) and Crondall (1658), and Cheshire contains an interesting group of churches and private chapels with particularly fine fittings, as at Cholmondeley, Tarvin and Prestbury. The churches at Shrivenham in Berkshire, Brampton Brian in Herefordshire and Compton Wynyates in Warwickshire were so damaged in the Civil War that they had to be rebuilt, the second in a red sandstone version of Perpendicular, the third with an odd blending of Gothic and Renaissance detail.

CIRCA 1660 TO 1820

The Restoration forms an arbitrary dividing line between the work of the Early Renaissance, with its tentative leanings to classicism but involuntary retention of the medieval arrangement, and the developed Late Renaissance style, with its classic sense of scale and proportion, its dignity and good taste. It is odd that so many writers, whose knowledge and appreciation of Gothic churches is sane and discriminating, have failed to grasp the peculiar charm and appropriateness of these later productions, which reflect so admirably the individualism and churchmanship of their times. Their range of craftsmanship, at its best comparable with the finest work of the Middle Ages, has suffered disastrously at the hands of meddlesome Gothicising architects, parsons, and landlords; and even nowadays the episcopal bench is often not altogether immune from the old anti-Renaissance prejudice, as may be judged from its recent ill-judged advocacy of proposals for the demolition of some of the finer City churches.

The revolution in church design effected towards the close of the seventeenth century was largely brought about by one

79 GLYNDE, SUSSEX (*circa* 1700)

78 BLANDFORD, DORSET: By John Bastard (1732)

RENAISSANCE CHURCH EXTERIORS

80 TYBERTON, HEREFORDSHIRE (1720)

81 ST. PAUL'S WALDEN, HERTFORDSHIRE
(circa 1750)

RENAISSANCE CHURCH INTERIORS

man, Sir Christopher Wren, whose rebuilding of the City of London churches after the Great Fire created a new conception of usage and arrangement and a new standard of ornament. It is impossible in this study, which must necessarily confine itself chiefly to Gothic churches, to do justice to this remarkable gallery of examples achieved by a school of craftsmen working together almost intuitively under the inspiration of the master. Designed for Protestant worship and preaching, the chief characteristic of these churches was a rich and decorous simplicity. Though their ranks had been thinned, a splendid group remained islanded in the commercial tide of the City, generally threatened by demolition but surely as worthy to be preserved as the husks of any earlier ruin. Now, alas, the bombing raids of 1939-41 have left but a slender remnant. There is no space for individual description, but the church lover is urged to make his pilgrimage to St. Margaret Pattens, St. James Garlickhithe, St. Benet Paul's Wharf, St. Magnus Martyr, London Bridge, St. Martin Ludgate, St. Margaret Lothbury and St. Mary at Hill, which at least have survived aerial attack. The dome is damaged at St. Stephen Walbrook (77).

Some delightful village churches of simpler type were also built under this influence, among them Willen in Buckinghamshire (1680), Gayhurst nearby (1728), Wolverton in Hampshire (1717), Blandford in Dorset (78) (1732) and Hopton Cangeford in Shropshire (*circa* 1700). In London and the larger towns, however, the Palladian influence was beginning to assert itself in the hands of such men as Gibbs at St. Martin-in-the-Fields and St. Mary le Strand, Hawksmoor at St. George's, Bloomsbury, and Christ Church, Spitalfields, and John James, who built St. George's, Hanover Square, and added the steeple to Hawksmoor's St. Alphege at his native Greenwich, now bombed. Such types are to be found in many provincial towns, such as Worcester, Bristol, Bath, and, at Shrewsbury, the circular St. Chad's—all the work of capable local designers; they persisted late into the eighteenth century, when we have the cult of literal classicism, as at Revett's Ayot St. Lawrence in Hertfordshire, and the Inwood's great church of St. Pancras, London, built in 1829 by composing pieces from several Greek monuments, curious but far from ineffective. There is also some restrained but well designed Regency work, as at Egham, St. John's, Waterloo Road, and Kennington, London, both raid-wrecked, St. Bartholomew's, Chichester, etc.

The more recent phases of church building can only be recapitulated very briefly. The Gothic Revival that followed immediately on the Classic had, of course, already been anticipated at an early period by Wren and others, as at St. Mary Aldermary and St. Dunstan-in-the-East, both gutted. Sporadic essays in Gothic, often delicate and refined, continued throughout the eighteenth century, as at Croome, Shobdon, Hartwell and Tetbury. Without going the lengths of certain amateurs who have made a cult of early nineteenth-century Revival Gothic, it can be conceded that the essays of 1800–1830 have often individual grace in design, and are well proportioned and appropriately thought out, e.g. Rickman's Ombersley, Worcestershire, Belper and the fabrics of a number of Midland and Northern towns. But it was not until the second quarter of the nineteenth that the dams were unloosed to admit a troubled flood, of which only the present century has seen the ebb. The first phase of the Revival was largely an attenuated version of Perpendicular that can be studied without emotion in James Savage's St. Luke's, Chelsea, and Vulliamy's Christ Church, Woburn Square, among others. In the hands of A. W. Pugin and his followers the movement attained something of the fervour of a crusade, and London and the provinces were soon producing a mushroom crop of Gothic towers and spires that sought to emulate, if it failed to achieve, the splendours of the marshlands and of the Nene Valley. Scholarly and correct as they are, these productions of the 'sixties and 'seventies seem as removed from the spirit of Gothic architecture as a Victorian Sabbath from a fifteenth-century Palm Sunday. In this culminating phase the thirteenth century was generally the criterion aimed at, and irreparable damage was done to many ancient fabrics by efforts to wipe out the blot of later centuries and restore the fancied characteristics of that period.

Nevertheless, it is easy to criticise the work of the later nineteenth century too harshly. Architects of the calibre of J. L. Pearson and Gilbert Scott the younger were able to produce work of individuality and distinction, as at St. Augustine's, Kilburn, and St. Agnes', Kennington, respectively. Similarly, it must not be forgotten that in restoration these men were often magnificent surveyors, and their work both necessary and instrumental in preserving tired fabrics for posterity.

Now the tide has turned, and freed from the influence of Revivalism, architects are striving with a fair measure of success to establish a type of church building in line with modern needs, based on a sensitive use of the materials now available and an appreciation of their resources. Restoration is becoming more tolerant and informed, and a real advance has been made in the education of the public taste towards a better appreciation of the English heritage of parish churches.

CHAPTER FOUR

Features and Fittings of Parish Churches

THIS chapter attempts to condense into a few pages the contents of a considerable library of antiquarian research and study. The sub-sections into which it is divided can only give the briefest outlines of their subjects, and are intended to awaken an interest in matters which will repay much more serious investigation. These subjects, to be properly appreciated, should be studied as they apply to the whole range of church architecture, including minster, collegiate and cathedral, as well as parish, churches. While in many of their features the latter were necessarily the poor relations of the greater buildings, in a few they were supreme—as in wooden screens, and, in fact, in almost every department of woodwork design with the exception of stalls. Parish church fittings cover an immense range that can only be superficially indicated, and the same applies to tombs and monuments, which, if they failed to achieve the costly magnificence of much cathedral work, form an inexhaustible treasury of craftsmanship, heraldry and social history.

TOWERS, SPIRES AND STEEPLES (*v.* also p. 39)

The function, position and planning of parish church towers has been touched upon briefly. Saxon examples, of which some eighty remain in whole or in part about the country, were, as has been seen, fairly severe structures of crude masonry, only relieved by the quoining at their angles (usually of long-and-short type), by their groups of round- or triangular-headed windows, and, occasionally, by the application of light pilaster-strips, as at Earl's Barton and Barton-on-Humber. Often rising to seventy feet or more, there is generally real dignity in their rough-hewn austerity, in which collectively may be recognised one of the earliest monuments of English art. There is no space to quote a comprehensive list, but the examples at Clapham in Bedfordshire, St. Peter-at-Gowts at Lincoln, Monkwearmouth in Durham, Barnack and Earl's Barton (82) in Northamptonshire, Deerhurst in Gloucestershire and Bishopstone in Sussex comprise a representative group.

As opposed to Saxon practice, a tall belfry tower was never a marked feature of Anglo-Norman design. Those that were built were of three types: central over a cruciform church, central over the chancel of a three-cell church, and western. The central towers were for the most part short and sturdy, as at Newhaven and Melbourne (heightened at a later date), though exceptions occur to this rule, as at St. John's at Devizes (30), Old Shoreham (42), and the fine structure at Castor in Northamptonshire, with its three tiers of rich arcading. Western towers on a grand scale were similarly rare, the usual types being low, plain and square on plan, or as is so often found in East Anglia, circular, carrying on a pre-Conquest tradition of the district. This form, as has been seen, was largely dictated by economy to obviate the use of dressed stones for quoins, the material being the local flint, as at Thorpe and Haddiscoe in Norfolk and Herringfleet in Suffolk.

The earliest tower-coverings were of two types—the "saddleback," of which a fair number of examples remain, facing in both possible directions, as at Sarratt in Hertfordshire, Wadenhoe in Northamptonshire and Elm in Somerset; and the pyramid, as at Clymping and many other churches in Sussex, Sarnesfield in Herefordshire and Godmersham in Kent. The latter type, built of wood and covered with tiles, was the direct precursor of the Gothic spire, which developed from it by rapid stages early in the thirteenth century. In the first of these, the pyramid was merely heightened and chamfered at the four angles, as may still be seen in many towers, such as Merstham in Surrey (124) and Preston in Kent. This essentially timber construction was soon imitated in stone to a fair height, as at Etton and Denford in Northamptonshire. From thence it was a short step to the developed octagonal broach spire, which in certain districts formed so grand a feature of the thirteenth- and earlier fourteenth-century styles.

With the thirteenth century, the tower and spire became an integral and unified composition. The towers themselves varied in richness, being arranged in stages of lancet windows and arcading between string-courses, with buttressing at the angles. The spire often rose from a crowning cornice carried on corbel-tables, the transition from the square to the octagon being effected on the outside by plain triangular masses of masonry, called "broaches," and on the inside by squinch-arches across the angles. Often rising to a hundred and fifty feet or more, Early English broach spires were aesthetically as well as structurally one of the supreme achievements of their age, their purity of outline expressing perfectly the grave austerity so typical of thirteenth-century art and religious feeling. Variety in design was achieved simply enough by the

82 EARL'S BARTON, NORTHAMPTONSHIRE: The venerable
Saxon Tower with its Stonework Patterning

83   OLNEY, BUCKINGHAMSHIRE : The Tower and pinnacled
Broach Spire of Cowper's Church

84 ST. LEONARD'S, SHOREDITCH, LONDON : Showing the Renaissance
Steeple and West Front. By George Dance (1741)

85 KETTON, RUTLAND: The Broach Construction of the Thirteenth Century

86 HIGHAM FERRERS, NORTHAMPTONSHIRE: The Parapet Construction of the Fourteenth Century

SPIRES OF THE STONE BELT

number and arrangement of the dormer-like spire windows, set beneath delicate projecting gables; nevertheless, the plainest are often the most pleasing, where the effect relies entirely on nicety of proportion. The distribution of these spires is much localised—a subject dealt with in the next chapter—and while it is difficult to make a choice of examples, mention must be made of Threckingham, North Raunceby and St. Mary's at Stamford in Lincolnshire, Ketton in Rutland (85), Alconbury and Warboys (134) in Huntingdonshire, and Raunds, Luddington and Barnwell St. Andrew in Northamptonshire, which are definitely among the most striking.

Though chiefly characteristic of the thirteenth century, the broach spire, particularly in its home districts, persisted well into the fourteenth, when crocketing sometimes enriched the angles and window gables. Broadly speaking, this construction began to be superseded at about the turn of the century by a second type, in which the broach was discarded, the junction of spire and tower being masked by an ornamental parapet enclosing a platform, from which, incidentally, repairs could easily be effected. This parapet, usually with pinnacles at the four corners and occasionally with flying-buttresses to the spire, became an increasingly decorative feature as the century advanced. Towers themselves also grew richer, their tabernacle-work now incorporating the favourite ogee motive, with the crocket and ballflower in their myriads. At its best, the effect was one of rich and subtle elegance, as may be judged in such examples as Grantham and Louth in Lincolnshire (9), St. Michael's at Coventry, Patrington in Yorkshire (45), Kettering in Northamptonshire, and many another great church in the stone districts.

So far as towers were concerned, the fifteenth century remained the supreme building period, providing one of the major English contributions to medieval art. Dignified by their beauty of proportion, Perpendicular church towers show everywhere the same imaginative flexibility on the part of their builders, though they represent many different schools of local design working in various materials according to the resources of districts. Ranging in height from some fifty to nearly three hundred feet, they pass from the dignified severity of Bishop's Nympton in Devon, St. Neots in Cornwall (142) and Sall in Norfolk, to the extremes of panelled richness to be found at St. Mary's at Taunton, Ilminster and Leigh-on-Mendip in Somerset, and All Saints (now the cathedral) at Derby. Some rise in absolute simplicity to a sumptuous crowning storey, as at Tickhill in Yorkshire, while in others the ornament is checked until the final battlements and pinnacles, where it bursts forth in a riot of fretted stonework, as at Dundry in Somerset and Thornbury in Gloucestershire (133). Some of the loveliest, however, whether plain or ornate, are those most uniform in texture, such as Wrexham, where the diapering is carried evenly through each storey. Most are square on plan, but the octagonal type is by no means infrequent, particularly for central towers, as at Doulting in Somerset (44). Others are crowned by an octagonal lantern

of one or more storeys, surrounded by a parapet and occasionally supported by flying-buttresses, as at Colyton in Devon, Fotheringay and Lowick in Northamptonshire, and the *tour-de-force* of St. Botolph's at Boston (4), rising like a slender finger above the long levels of the Wash.

In smaller churches, where there was often no tower or belfry accommodation, the bells were swung in turrets of stone, brick or timber above the western gable. In its design at least, Preston in Gloucestershire provides an excellent example of a village bellcote, though here the turret is placed over the chancel arch, in the position generally occupied during the later Middle Ages by the sanctus bell, which was rung at the Elevation in the celebration of Mass. The standard Midland type of stone bellcote, as at Manton in Rutland, has two openings, and is appropriate enough, if a little awkward for three

BELLCOTE, PRESTON,
GLOUCESTERSHIRE

bells. The West Country showed far more originality and variety in its cage-like structures, as may be well seen at Harescombe in Gloucestershire (123) and Brympton in Somerset. But it was the little "shingled" bellcote in timber that was most typical of the smaller English country church. This occurs in all shapes and sizes, from the one-bell cotes with tiny roofs of Coates and Ford in Sussex to the real timber towers of Mountnessing in Essex and Great Bookham in Surrey (48); while a few show pleasant touches of half-timber, as at Vowchurch and Hope Bagot in Herefordshire. The spirelets really constitute the "timber broach" construction in miniature; most are short and sturdy, as at

Litlington in Sussex (122), though some, like Laindon in Essex and Thursley in Surrey, are quite tall and slender. From these, it was only a stage further to take the belfry outside the walls and obtain structures as picturesque and original as the Essex group (*vide* p. 101) or Brookland on Romney Marsh, where a large timber belfry of "candle-snuffer" design stands detached on the ground beside the church.

This section would be incomplete without some mention of the beautiful steeples of the Renaissance churches which began to rise over the English towns and cities soon after the Great Fire of London had gained admission for Wren's exquisite fertility of design. These, notwithstanding their purely classical detail, must be regarded as the generic descendants of the medieval spires. Without exact parallel abroad at their period, their evolution reflected the innate conservatism of Englishmen, among whom tradition dies hard and compromise is the food of life. Here, indeed, was a compromise between the medieval and the classic with an individual beauty of its own. The silvery Portland stone first used at about this time was an ideal material for its construction, and from any vantage point in the City of London the vista of Renaissance steeples, even if sadly reduced, provides an unforgettable experience, one that almost literally interprets the old catch-phrase "a symphony in stone."

PORCHES AND DOORWAYS (*v.* also p. 41)

The forms of Saxon and Norman doorways were discussed briefly in the last chapter. As has been seen, a striking feature of the developed Anglo-Norman style was the importance given to the entrances of even modest country churches such as Adel and Iffley. The south doorway of the nave, usually the principal entrance, was singled out for special treatment, as in the cases of Kilpeck (55) and St. Margaret-at-Cliffe. Examples also occur of rich western doorways, as at Barfreston, Castle Rising and again at Iffley, where they form integral features of quite considerable frontal compositions.

The same care for doorway design continued through the thirteenth century, though now a porch was often added, a feature previously confined mainly to larger churches. Early English porches vary somewhat in design, the more usual type projecting boldly beneath a steep-pitched gable, with ranges of simple arcading, as at Barnack. Occasionally they were roofed with stone vaulting, while the doorways, built in recessed orders, displayed the dog-tooth and stiff-leaf

M

carving in the capitals. A rarer type can be seen at Skelton, where the south porch is of quite shallow projection, in fact little more than a single portal of multiple recessed orders beneath a gable, heavily carved. Shallow recessed western porches of rather similar type occur at Raunds and Higham Ferrers, the latter with a double entrance surrounded by remarkable lunettes of figure-carving. At Warmington in the same neighbourhood, the thirteenth-century church has doorways both north and south, with particularly fine foliage in the capitals.

The fourteenth century brought its usual intensification of ornament into porches, introducing the ogee arch, the cusp, the crocket and the ballflower, which were used with gallant effect at Bampton in Oxfordshire and Little Addington in Northamptonshire. Some examples, however, like Patrington, are of comparatively plain design. On the outside, niches were supplied for saint-carvings, as at Heckington, and on the inside holy-water stoups were now invariably provided. Heckington can be cited as perhaps the most beautiful of Decorated porches, rich and lovely in each of its delicate features. Even the small priests' doors on the south sides of chancels were now ornamentally treated, as in the graceful examples at Crick in Northamptonshire and Walcot in Lincolnshire.

As with towers, the fifteenth century saw the culmination of porch design in this country; the period offers an array of types in different materials that makes a brief analysis rather inadequate. Porches were often now, as has been seen, of two or more storeys, enriched with pinnacles, battlements and pierced parapets, with niches and canopies for saint-carvings, heraldic badges, stone panelling for surface decoration, and in East Anglia the delicate diapering of flint flushwork. St. Nicholas' at King's Lynn (88), Eye (144) and Southwold in Suffolk, Northleach in the Cotswolds, Tiverton in Devon (70), Pulham St. Mary in Norfolk, and St. Botolph's at Boston may be chosen almost at random from among the stateliest examples. At Bruton in Somerset, the north porch is as high as the towers of many churches, at Ludlow the south porch is hexagonal, while Boxford in Suffolk incorporates exceptional examples in both stone and wood. The latter material was much used for porches, particularly in the South-East, and produced its own type of structure, as at Aconbury in Herefordshire (90), South Hayling and Warblington in Hampshire, and Benfleet in Essex. Examples in molded brick are of fairly common occurrence, particularly in East Anglia, as at Feering and Sandon (127) in Essex and Winston in Suffolk.

88 ST. NICHOLAS', KING'S LYNN, NORFOLK :
An East Anglian *Tour de Force*

87 CROWCOMBE, SOMERSET : West Country type

PORCHES OF THE FIFTEENTH CENTURY

90   ACONBURY, HEREFORDSHIRE: The Timber
West Porch (late Fifteenth Century)

89   EAST DEREHAM, NORFOLK: A "Seven
Sacraments" Font of the Fifteenth Century

EXTERIOR STONEWORK

Practically nothing can be said here of the features and details of exterior stonework to be found in most parish churches, on which the mason lavished the beauty and skill of his craft—the buttresses, with their later panelling; the parapets, battlements, and crestings; the finials, gargoyles, and gable crosses. Their variety was inexhaustible, and is touched upon briefly under other headings, e.g. the pierced openwork parapets of Somerset (3) and Heckington (121), the richness of Tiverton (70) and St. John's at Devizes (30), the exuberant carving of such a church as St. Mary Magdalene at Launceston. But a word must be added on the subject of gargoyles, or drain-heads, in which the medieval feeling for the grotesque found one of its most graphic expressions. Amazing is the range of curious beasts, contorted figures and demoniac faces that scowl or grin from the parapets of English churches. There is a remarkable array of them in the Mendip district, as at Burrington, and another in the fourteenth-century churches of Lincolnshire that rivals the grotesques of the almost contemporary Luttrell Psalter. This was an odd province of church craftsmanship, in which the productions were for once not collective but utterly individual.

VAULTS AND ROOFS

The use of stone vaulting in parish churches was exceptional, and for the most part confined to larger buildings. It is found, however, in a fair number of Norman chancels. occasionally groined, as at Coln St. Denis in the Cotswolds, but more frequently of quadripartite ribbed type, as at Kilpeck, Elkstone (54) and Hemel Hempstead. The chancel of Tickencote is a unique example of a Norman sexpartite vault. When there was an apse, this was also generally vaulted, as at Kilpeck, Compton in Surrey and St. Mary's at Guildford.

Examples of Transitional vaulting occur in the aisles of New Shoreham and elsewhere. To the thirteenth century belong the nave vault of the same church and the chancel vaults of Minster in Thanet and Crondall in Hampshire; to the fourteenth, the fine lierne coverings at St. Mary Redcliffe at Bristol and Nantwich in Cheshire. It should be pointed out, however, that most of these churches were of collegiate status for long periods of their history, while the latter two at least were of a splendour beyond the range of the average parish building. With the fifteenth century, fan-vaulting on a small scale was sometimes used with delicate effect for aisles and chapels, as at North Leigh in Oxfordshire and Cullompton and Ottery St. Mary in Devon. It was also as will be seen much applied, in wood or stone, to tomb canopies, testers, screens and other features, but above all to the interiors of porches and towers, of which a great range of examples survives all over the country.

The national and almost universal type of parish church

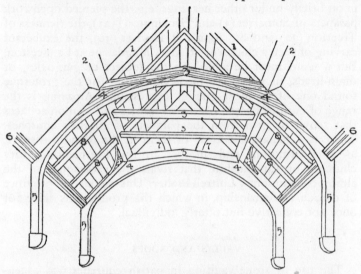

PARTS OF AN ARCH-BRACED ROOF
(With Collar-beams on the Common Rafters: St. Mary's, Leicester)

1, 1. Principals	5, 5. Wall-posts
2, 2. Purlins	6, 6. Wall-plates
3, 3. Collar-beams	7, 7. Struts
4, 4. Arch-braces	8, 8. Common Rafters

covering, however, was the timber roof—a form of construction in which the English excelled, and of which, in spite of the perishable nature of the material and the often ill-judged restoration work of the last century, a splendid gallery of examples remains. Limited space precludes a full survey of the construction, classification, and character of the different types, which suffer considerably in their literature from a confused and confusing nomenclature. Two main groups, however, may be distinguished—the *beam* type, and the *coupled* or *rafter* type, with its two series of inclined timbers meeting at the apex of the gable. The chief parts of the medieval roof are named in the accompanying diagrams. Their struc-

tural and decorative elaboration was primarily due to the
insertion of strengthening devices to prevent spreading,
sagging or other movement. If such devices were applied
separately to each rafter the roof is called *single-framed*. If, by
the most usual and economical method, the devices occur
at intervals, perhaps one to a bay, the roof is *double-framed*.
The chief rafters bearing the devices are the *principals*, and
the timbers between them the *common rafters*. The horizontal
purlins provide longitudinal stiffening, and vary from one to
three in a slope.

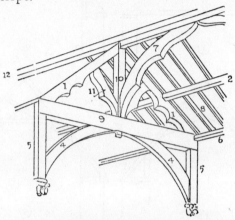

PARTS OF A KING-POST ROOF
(Adderbury, Oxfordshire)

1, 1. Principal Rafters	7. Longitudinal Strut
2. Purlin	8. Common Rafter
4, 4. Arch-braces (under Tie-beam)	9. Tiebeam
5, 5. Wall-posts	10. King-post
6. Wall-plate	11. Strut

12. Ridge Piece

The *beam* type was chiefly used for the lean-to roofs of
aisles, occasionally with curved spandrel-like braces, as at
Southacre. The *coupled* type was from quite early times
strengthened by *tie-beams* between the walls at the foot of the
rafters, making a triangular section. The tie-beams themselves were sometimes reinforced underneath by triangular
or arched bracing-pieces, as at Mildenhall, while the apex was
connected with the middle of the tie-beams by *king-posts*,
sometimes, as at Adderbury, with several branches. Two or
more posts connecting the tie-beams with the gable produced
the *queen-post* type, as at Gedney and Addlethorpe.
Another strengthening arrangement was the insertion of

collars or *collar-beams* between the rafters, at varying heights
in the gable. Intersecting beams placed diagonally produced
the *scissor-beam* roof, rare in England. Ultra-cautious builders

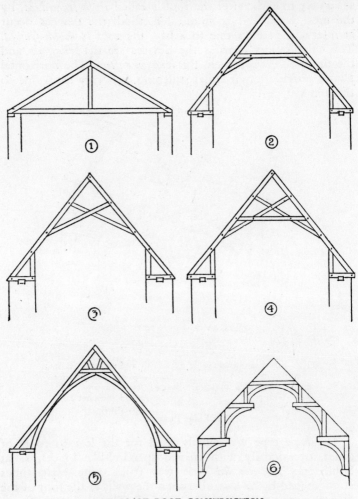

TYPES OF ROOF CONSTRUCTION

1. King-post
3. Scissor-beam
5. Arch-braced

2. Collar-beam and Braces
4. Collar with Scissor-beams
6. Double Hammer-beam

occasionally inserted a straight collar as well, and a rare
job it must have been to fit, and a rare tangle the finished
result appeared.

If, instead of the two braces being straight, they were curved

91　MARCH, CAMBRIDGESHIRE : The Double-Hammerbeam Roof,
with its Galaxy of Carved Angels (Fifteenth Century)

92　HIGHER BICKINGTON, DEVON : Carved Bench-Ends,
Late Gothic and Early Renaissance

94   DEAN, BEDFORDSHIRE : Depressed
Tiebeam Type

FIFTEENTH-CENTURY TIMBER ROOFS

93   NECTON, NORFOLK : Alternating Hammerbeam
and Arched Brace Type

in shape, and connected to form a segmental arch, the important and widespread *arched brace* roof was the result, as at Westhall and Pulham Magdalen; very occasionally this was completely boarded over, as in the Southwold nave. If the arch-braces were substantial enough, the collar was sometimes omitted; again, to give more space and a better shape to the braces, their feet were brought down to a horizontal post, or *hammer-beam*, projecting from the wall, producing a type of roof which, structurally as well as decoratively, became one of the glories of English carpentry (91). Sometimes the process was carried out in two stages, producing the *double hammer-beam* type, of which Knapton and March (91) are such superb examples. If, however, instead of an arch-brace to each principal there was a curved brace to most or all of the rafters, the *wagon* or *barrel-shaped* roof, so popular in the South-West, was obtained, generally plastered between the timbers (140), but occasionally boarded over.

These, very briefly, were the chief roof types, but the medieval craftsman, despising formulæ, produced a crop of hybrids, combinations and variants which it would need a full chapter to enumerate. There was, for instance, the East Anglian fashion of fitting each principal in turn with a tie-beam or hammer-beam (as at Walsham-le-Willows), or else of alternating a hammer-beam with an arched brace, as at Necton (93). The former construction possibly lends slight colour to the theory that the hammer-beam was in reality a tie-beam with the middle cut out, though chronology seems to oppose the idea.

It remains to consider two individual types of tie-beam roof of low pitch. If the rafters were only a short distance above the tie-beam, i.e. the "triangle" was a low one, the space was sometimes filled with wooden tracery, generally of more decorative than structural significance, though sometimes it might incorporate and combine both a king- and queen-post. This was a style most typical of Somerset and Devon, as at Martock and St. Cuthbert's at Wells (49). Sometimes, to give greater strength, the tie-beam was cambered, i.e. sloped upwards in the centre, as in the Trinity Chapel at Cirencester. If the tie-beam was cut solid and the roof further flattened, so as to decrease still more the height of the "triangle," the rafters could rest directly upon it, producing a fine later type favoured in most districts, as at Dean (94), Ewelme, Lavenham (35) and elsewhere. The almost flat pitch of the last phase called for the use of lead as an outer covering, and its weight, with that of the tie-beam and all, could be supported by arched braces well brought down by wall-posts. This type may be called the *solid tie-beam*, or simply the *beam* roof. It occurs in the south aisle of St. Martin's at Leicester as early as the end of the thirteenth century, but the majority of examples date from the later fifteenth. In the North and in Wales the undersides were often sub-divided into a multiplicity of small panels, finely carved, and rather resembling the "coffering" of classic architecture, as at Ruthin.

Such were the main structural varieties of English medieval timber roofing. Of Norman date little now remains, but it may be assumed that the churches of that period were principally tied together by great oak beams, with simple trussed rafter roofs above. With the thirteenth century, however, the possibilities of open timber roofing began to grow on the imaginations of the builders. Now the roofs were generally high in pitch and acutely pointed, as in the naves of Long Stanton in Cambridgeshire and Filby in Norfolk, which are both excellent examples of the trussed rafter type. Towards the close of the century the pitch began to decrease, and with the fourteenth became universally lower; good examples of Decorated roofing survive at Starston in Norfolk, at Adderbury (p. 75) and at Higham Ferrers. But the fifteenth century was the period of greatest development, which saw most of the innovations detailed in the preceding pages. Now the pitch was often almost flat, as at St. Neots and Buckden in Huntingdonshire, Marston Moretaine and Dean in Bedfordshire (94), and in many another fine Perpendicular example.

The two considerable exceptions to the later prevalence of the obtuse roof can be studied in the South-West and in the East of England respectively. In the first, which occurred throughout Cornwall, in many parts of Devon and Somerset, and occasionally in Dorset and Hampshire, the roofs were of the coved *wagon* type already described, their light intersecting timbers dividing them up into symmetrical panels. The medieval plan was to lath, plaster and whitewash the underside of the roof, thus lightening the unclerestoried interior and showing up the beauty of the carving. Unfortunately, the restorers have now often cleaned away the plaster, and instead of leaving the rafters exposed, have covered them with planed boards, often of pitch pine. Some of these roofs, however, were boarded over from the first, as in the richly ornamented example at Cullompton.

The second variation was the *hammer-beam* type already described—an essentially fifteenth-century innovation, though

a few earlier examples are possible. This offered splendid
facilities for ornamental treatment. Sometimes there was open
tracery in the triangular spaces between the hammer-beams
and the rafters, as at Blakeney and Trunch, with often a deep
and richly carved cornice beneath. Arched braces ran length-
wise between the wall-posts, generally carved and sometimes
bearing angels with outspread wings, as at Necton (93).
Carved angels appeared in their galaxies in certain later
churches; their effect, in the full blaze of the original colouring,
can only be imagined, and even now there are few things in
English medieval art to compare with the upward rush of
wings in such famous and splendid double hammer-beam
roofs as those at Knapton in Norfolk, Woolpit in Suffolk,
and, above all, March in Cambridgeshire (91), which alone
incorporates over a hundred angels.

The hammer-beam construction lingered in a number of
Renaissance survivals (p. 64), to which might be added South
Harting in Sussex, which dates from 1574, the chancel roof of
Huyton in Lancashire, built as late as 1663, and Plaxtole in Kent
and Brampton Brian in Herefordshire (mid. 17th c.); in the same
county Vowchurch (1613) is of tiebeam type. Post-Restoration
churches were invariably provided with rich plaster ceilings,
mostly of excellent craftsmanship in the style of their periods,
as at King Charles the Martyr at Tunbridge Wells, St. Clement
Danes in London and in most of Wren's City churches.

FITTINGS IN STONE

Inside the parish church, the most conspicuous stone
fittings to-day are often the fonts. These cover a wide range
of styles and periods, and while many were singled out for
special treatment, others remain so unassuming and simple
that it is difficult to gauge their period with any certainty.
They were generally placed at the west ends of naves, and
took the form of cylindrical, octagonal or square bowls,
usually enriched with panels of geometrical or figure carving,
supported on central stone stems, sometimes with free-standing
shafts. Some of the Norman fonts are strikingly carved, and
convey a good idea of the more intimate craftsmanship of their
period, as at Chaddesley Corbet in Worcestershire, Coleshill in
Warwickshire and Winster in Derbyshire. Of the famous
black Tournai marble type, five are parochial, three of them in
Hampshire, of which perhaps the finest is at St. Mary Bourne.

Many characteristic examples of the thirteenth and fourteenth centuries have survived, but the grandest productions
were of the fifteenth, especially in East Anglia, where many

N

were raised on steps and carved with delicate figuring, perhaps incorporating panels of the Seven Sacraments, as at East Dereham in Norfolk (89). During the Early Renaissance phase their design changed little, but after the Restoration a pleasing type was evolved appropriate to the character of the new churches, generally in the form of marble bowls decorated with winged cherubs' heads.

The craftsmanship of pulpits was often similarly striking, though this feature was more often carried out in wood. Such stone examples as survive seldom date from earlier than *circa* 1380, their typical decoration being the cusped stone panelling of their period, as at Long Coombe in Oxfordshire and Nantwich in Cheshire. Pulpit canopies in stone survive in two churches, Arundel in Sussex and Cold Ashton in Gloucestershire. A Devon type was very elaborately carved with figures in niches and heavy foliage reminiscent of local wood forms, as at Dittisham and Witheredge. Stone lecterns are rare; the finest are the richly carved examples of the thirteenth century at Crowle and Norton in Worcestershire, the latter brought from Evesham Abbey. Stone book-brackets, however, were occasionally fitted in the chancel wall, particularly among the Derbyshire churches.

The greatest range of stone fittings was reserved for the chancel. While the majority of surviving screens are of wood, a fair number of stone examples are to be seen, mostly of the fourteenth and fifteenth centuries, particularly in Wiltshire. The earlier ones consist of a simple arrangement of three arches, as at Bottisham in Cambridgeshire and Bamford in Suffolk; the later and richer productions hankered after the wood-carver's technique, particularly in their treatment of tracery and detail—there is a fine example of Devon type at Totnes. Sedilia—the triple canopied priests' seats on the south side of chancels—occurred at every period, but were at their richest during the Decorated phase of the fourteenth century, which produced such pinnacled *tours-de-force* as those at Hawton in Nottinghamshire and Heckington in Lincolnshire, with their rich carving in capitals, canopies and spandrels. There are good Perpendicular examples at Adderbury in Oxfordshire and St. Mary's at Oxford, and an amusing Renaissance variant at Wymondham in Norfolk.

Sometimes the sedilia formed a single composition with the piscina, or drain for washing the sacred vessels, which was then accorded a similar canopied treatment. This, where in a chancel, was on the east side of the sedilia; its presence in other parts of the church, as at the eastern ends of aisles or

96 LAVENHAM, SUFFOLK: The rich Screenwork
of the Sprying Family Pew

95 HAWTON, NOTTINGHAMSHIRE: The
Fourteenth-century Easter Sepulchre

97 BAMPTON, OXFORDSHIRE : The Sculptured Reredos

98 LUDLOW, SHROPSHIRE : Misericord: a Fireside Scene

99 LONG MELFORD, SUFFOLK : Alabaster Relief of the Life
of the Virgin

in transepts, indicates a former altar. On the north side of the chancel was often an Easter Sepulchre, or richly canopied recess of fourteenth-century or later date, built to accommodate the Host and altar crucifix during the period of fast and vigil from Good Friday to Easter morning. The lower panels were sometimes carved with reliefs of sleeping men-at-arms, representing the Roman soldiers guarding the Sepulchre; the upper ones with scenes of the Resurrection. Here, again, the richest examples are Decorated, with Hawton (95) and Heckington at the summit of achievement.

While most of the stone altars were thrown down at the Reformation, a number are in existence about the country, though rarely *in situ*, consisting of plain slabs incised with consecration crosses at the four corners and in the centre. The beautiful stone reredoses that adorned so many churches were similarly mishandled, which is not surprising, since they were the vehicles of the most delicate canopy-work and carving. Sometimes the rows of empty niches remain, as in the Patrington Lady Chapel; or a mutilated framework may allow in the mind's eye a reconstruction of a once beautiful *ensemble*, as in the aisle chapels at St. Cuthbert's at Wells. Of the few that remain untouched, mention may be made of that at Drayton in Berkshire, with its carved relief of the Life of the Virgin, no longer in its original position, the canopied Last Supper at Somerton in Oxfordshire, dug up unspoilt from the churchyard, and the rather similar work at Bampton in Oxfordshire (97). These productions were usually "shopwork" in the famous English craft of alabaster carving, which has now almost entirely vanished from our churches, though many of its stock panels, such as the Resurrection (2) and the Life of the Virgin (99), can be seen individually in museums both in this country and on the Continent.

FITTINGS IN WOOD

Woodwork fittings cover a wide range. English craftsmen seem to have been at their happiest working in this material, and it is a matter for congratulation that such a wealth of their productions has come down to us largely unscathed either by the disorders of the Reformation or the mishandling of the last century.

Doors have survived in great numbers, ranging from plain examples in stout oak, bare of ornament save for that applied by the smith, to the intricacies of traceried panelling found in such churches as St. Botolph's at Boston, Wellow in

Somerset and St. Nicholas' at King's Lynn. Inside the church, the font-cover is often a very striking feature of the nave. Though no example is known of earlier date than the fourteenth century, its design was capable of some variation within two main types. Of these, the first was the so-called *triptych*, which remained fixed and opened like a cupboard; in the second the cover could be lifted from the font outright by a counterweight and pulley. At its simplest, this feature consisted of little more than a plain wooden pyramid, after the Renaissance generally of ogee form; but during the fifteenth century it often achieved an astonishing elaboration, its forest of pinnacles and canopies rising spire-like almost to the roof, as at Ufford (100). Other sumptuous examples of similar type can be seen at Halifax in Yorkshire (101), Worlingworth in Suffolk, North Walsham in Norfolk, Ewelme in Oxfordshire and Frieston in Lincolnshire. Thaxted in Essex (60) and Swymbridge in Devon belong to a group in which the font itself is entirely enclosed by a timber framework, while at Trunch in Norfolk it stands beneath a delicate *baldachino* of two storeys. Some later Perpendicular font-covers, such as those at Swymbridge and Terrington St. Clement, incorporate definite Renaissance motives, but in many Jacobean examples, as at Astbury in Cheshire, Walpole St. Peter in Norfolk and Bishop Cosin's woodwork in some of the churches of the Durham Diocese, the old forms remain beneath a veneer of the new detail.

Much craftsmanship was bestowed on the seating of churches, particularly on bench-ends, which were of two main types—either traceried, or panelled with carving in relief. As a crowning feature there was often a *poupée*-head to each, either in the form of a trefoil of close-knit foliage, or carved with animals and figures. Of the first type, the best examples belong to two groups of the East and West respectively, as at Fressingfield, Woolpit and Harpley in East Anglia, Broomfield in Somerset, and High Bickington in Devon (92). In certain cases ships, windmills, tools and other subjects were incorporated, as at Bishop's Lydeard in Somerset and Altarnun and other churches in Cornwall. Of bench-ends with figure-carving, the finest ranges, though mutilated, are at Wiggenhall St. Mary the Virgin (102) and Wiggenhall St. Germans in the Norfolk Fens, with their series of the Seven Deadly Sins and Seven Sacraments, and fine rows of *poupée*-heads.

Family pews are mostly of Early Renaissance design, as at Holcombe Rogus in Devon and the Rycote Chapel in Oxfordshire; at Kedington in Suffolk there is a fine example

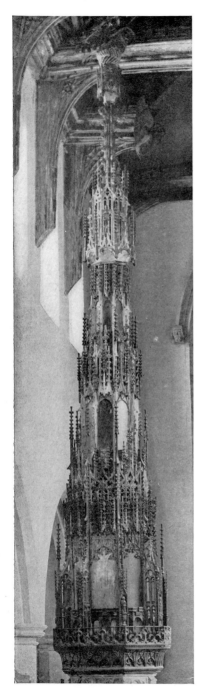 

100 UFFORD, SUFFOLK   101 HALIFAX, YORKSHIRE

LATE MEDIEVAL FONT-COVERS, EAST AND NORTH

103   NANTWICH, CHESHIRE : Carved Stallwork

102   WIGGENHALL ST. MARY-THE-VIRGIN,
NORFOLK : A Figured Bench-end

FIFTEENTH-CENTURY WOODWORK

105. ST. WOOLOS, NEWPORT, MONMOUTH-
SHIRE (now the Cathedral) : The Norman Nave

104. SOUTH BURLINGHAM, NORFOLK : Fifteenth-
century Screen and Pulpit, with Jacobean Canopy

106 PLYMTREE, DEVON: A typical late West Country Screen,
with painted figures in the lower panels

of medieval type. Chancel stalls, though more characteristic of minster and collegiate churches, are of occasional occurrence, a few with pinnacled canopies, as at Ludlow, Nantwich, Newark, and St. Margaret's at Lynn; but the majority are of the simple type of a fine Suffolk group that includes Southwold, Wingfield, Blythburgh, Dennington, and Fressingfield. Sometimes they are backed with panelling, and most incorporate attractive touches of carving in *poupée*-heads and elbows (103). The ends of chancel-stalls were generally richer than those of the congregational seating, and there are some good series of misericord carvings, as at Ludlow (98) and Southwold.

It is doubtful whether there are wooden pulpits of earlier date than the fifteenth century; but the later Middle Ages provide a great range of examples, mostly octagonal, with carved, traceried or painted panelling. Generally the carving is extremely fine, as at Rossington in Yorkshire and East Hagbourne in Berkshire; but the most elaborate work occurs in Somerset and Devon, where the craftsmanship runs riot in such examples as Ipplepen, Halberton, Dartmouth, Kenton and East Allington. Only some half-dozen medieval pulpit testers are known; probably the finest is at Edlesborough in Buckinghamshire, with its forest of pinnacles; but Renaissance testers were often added, as at South Burlingham in Norfolk (104). Early Renaissance examples are numerous and generally rather fine, with their sturdy panelling and carving and capacious sounding-boards. Those at Brancepeth in Durham, Newport in the Isle of Wight and Croscombe in Somerset (20) are as rich as any, the latter church with a magnificent range of Jacobean fittings to match. Late Renaissance pulpits can be very stately, as at St. Margaret's at Lynn and in the City churches; and the traditional "three-deckers" of the eighteenth century, combining in three tiers pulpit, lectern and clerk's seat, can still be seen in a few churches, as at Whitby in Yorkshire (23) and Sall in Norfolk.

While most medieval lecterns were of simple desk type, facing two ways or sometimes even four, a number were carved in the form of eagles with outspread wings—a type now stereotyped, perhaps over-frequently, in brass. Only one medieval organ-case is known, at Old Radnor in Wales, and this shows decided Renaissance influence. Those of the seventeenth and eighteenth centuries are often of great beauty, with their pierced carving, ornamental *putti* and trumpeting angels, as at Framlingham in Suffolk and again in the City churches. Post-Reformation communion tables were always of wood, and followed the styles of contemporary furniture; and the seventeenth and eighteenth centuries produced a delightful range of communion rails and chancel chairs—the latter including some of the earliest essays in revived Gothic. Other interesting features in wood are the Royal Arms, from Elizabeth to William IV, still to be found carved or painted in many country churches, dole-cupboards and bread-shelves in connection with charitable bequests, aumbries for the sacred vessels, of which a few medieval examples survive, and chests of every date and kind for money and documents, generally with marvellously intricate locks.

But the glory of English church woodwork was its screens, which in the course of about a century developed from modest beginnings to a richness and variety of design hardly equalled in any other sphere. There are none of importance earlier in date than the fourteenth century, and even then the work was still immature and hesitating compared with what was to follow, in a technique largely dependent upon stone forms. With the fifteenth century, the carpenter began decisively to assert himself, and to evolve a style suited to the working of his material. A book could be written on the varieties of local design in screens alone. It is only possible here to provide a bare *précis* of this attractive subject, treated in far more detail in Aymer Vallance's great monograph, *English Church Screens* and Howard and Crossley's *English Church Woodwork*, and to mention a few examples out of the hundreds still *in situ*.

A rough classification may be made into two main types. The first and simplest was the *square-framed* type, which occurred in most districts, but chiefly in the Midlands. This was generally built up with unpretentious tracery and panelling and appears characteristically at Higham Ferrers, Christian Malford in Wiltshire, Blore Ray in Staffordshire, and, in richer form, St. Mary's at Hitchin. In certain neighbourhoods it was overlaid with applied ogee ornament and tabernacle-work, as occurred largely in East Anglia, Lincolnshire, and Yorkshire, as at Dennington (107), Burgh and Kirksandal respectively.

The second type was the so-called *arched* screen, most characteristic of the West Country, but also sometimes found in East Anglia and the Midlands. In this, a crowning *bressummer*, or beam, projected like a canopy over the traceried openings, supported on timber vaulting of intricate design. This was by far the richer type, and in Devon attained an extraordinary elaboration, with multiple bands of openwork

107 DENNINGTON, SUFFOLK : The Screen and Rood-Loft

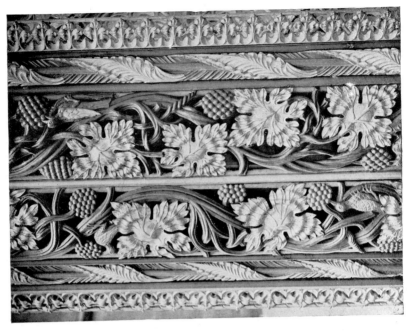

108 BOVEY TRACEY, DEVON : Carved Screen Detail

109 EATON BRAY, BEDFORDSHIRE : Thirteenth-century Wrought
Ironwork on a Door, by Thomas de Leighton

carving along the beams (108), delicate foliage between the ribs of the vaulting, and painted or richly carved wainscoting. The effect was enhanced in this district by the tremendous span of the screens from wall to wall, as at Cullompton and Bradninch. Other notable examples are at Lapford, Plymptree (106) and Atherington.

A variant almost exclusively confined to Wales had a wide gallery rood-loft above the bressummer, enriched with lace-like carving, as at St. Margaret's in Herefordshire. Rood-lofts, of course, survive occasionally in all districts, as at Atherington in Devon and Attleborough in Norfolk, but are nowhere so common. Their uses have already been touched upon, and it has been seen with what particular severity they were treated at the time of the Reformation. The Rood, with its statues, must certainly have been a spectacular feature of the pre-Reformation church, and the screen beneath it was usually gay with gilding and colour, traces of which may remain. Sometimes the lower panels were painted with saints and figures, particularly in East Anglia, where fine work can still be seen at Ranworth, Somerleyton (117) and other churches, as also, in a much broader technique, in Devon (118). Good screens were not infrequently added in the Renaissance styles, among which mention may be made of the Jacobean example at Croscombe (20), and the graceful Georgian structure at St. Paul's Walden in Hertfordshire (81).

FITTINGS IN METAL

Metals were never greatly employed in the equipment of parish churches, beyond the structural use of lead for covering roofs and spires, though the smith's art found an early expression in the decoration of wooden doors, the hinges and furniture of which were sometimes carried to the extremes of elaboration. While earlier Norman hinges were occasionally wrought with Viking-like effect, incorporating ships and dragons, as at Stillingfleet in Yorkshire, the twelfth century brought a more conventional treatment in boldly interlacing circles, as can be seen at Great Hormead in Hertfordshire and Skipwith in Yorkshire. With the thirteenth century came a graceful and distinctive foliated scrollwork, of which the two supreme examples, at Turvey and Eaton Bray in Bedford-shire (109), are the work of the great medieval smith, Thomas de Leighton, who made the Eleanor Grille at Westminster. After this century the metalwork of doors was mostly confined to a patterning of nail studs and well-wrought locks and key-plates.

Lead was sometimes used for fonts, which have a distinct form of their own in this material. The majority are of late Norman date, and incorporate seated figures in arcades, fabulous beasts and scrollwork. Wrought ironwork was used for tomb railings, sometimes with fine effect, as at Farleigh Hungerford in Somerset, but metal grilles, which may have been quite frequent, only survive in greater churches. It was only with the seventeenth and eighteenth centuries that metal screens and gates were used to fence off chapels and chancels, and some beautiful Renaissance work of this type is scattered about the country, notably in the churches of the Temple and St. Nicholas at Bristol, by William Edney, at Little Stanmore in Middlesex by an anonymous craftsman, and, perhaps finest of all, at All Saints (now the cathedral) at Derby, by the local master-smith, Robert Bakewell. Renaissance ironwork can also be seen in communion rails, sword and mace rests, hour-glass stands and other fittings— except the last named, generally in town churches.

The finest example of a medieval candelabrum in existence is that at the Temple Church at Bristol, but it is not a native work. Many parish churches about the country, however, are dignified by their gift candelabra of the seventeenth and eighteenth centuries, in brass, of which hundreds are to be seen, as in the West Country, at Ipplepen (31) and Wedmore (22).

TOMBS, MONUMENTS, AND BRASSES

For five centuries English craftsmanship devoted some of its finest efforts to tombs and monuments. There are few parish churches that do not contain some conspicuous work in this field, which, where the architectural interest is slight, may well constitute an attraction in itself to students of sculpture, costume or social history. The subject is one of such vastness and variety at every period that it can only be treated very cursorily, and churchyard monuments are of necessity completely ignored.

The earliest tombs to be seen in parish churches are the simple stone slabs of the twelfth century, incised with a wide range of foliated crosses. With the thirteenth century, the recumbent effigy made its first appearance, often in Purbeck marble, treated with an austere dignity typical of the material and the period, whether the figure is clad in priestly vestments or crusaders' armour. These effigies form a considerable subject in themselves, to which we owe much of our knowledge of English medieval figure-sculpture, dress, and armour, to

110 FRAMLINGHAM, SUFFOLK : Late Sixteenth-century Effigies of the Earl and Countess of Surrey

111 LOWICK, NORTHAMPTONSHIRE: Alabaster Effigies of
Ralp and Katheren Green, 1419

112 BLEWBURY, BERKSHIRE: A Squint

say nothing of heraldry and genealogy. With the fourteenth century, stone canopies were often placed over the effigies, on which the craftsmen concentrated some of their richest efforts. Now the groups grew less rigid and severe; we find the knight resting beside his lady, their hands still clasped, angels smoothing their pillow beneath a fretted head-canopy, and their favourite lapdogs at their feet (111).

From about the middle of the century, such tombs were generally, of course, productions of the craft workshops of the larger towns, notably Nottingham, the headquarters of the alabaster workers, whose art was famous throughout Europe. Though inevitably the work became more stereotyped during the fifteenth century, the standard remained high, and with their wide range of accessories and detail the tombs of this period well repay study. The sides of the slabs were now often panelled with delicate reliefs of "weepers" and other figures in tabernacle-work, and fan-vaulting was applied to the canopies, with rich heraldic cresting. It would be futile to cite examples from the vast output of this period, but certain churches are exceptionally well provided, as for instance Framlingham (110), Bottesford in Lincolnshire, Norbury, Elford, Warkton in Northamptonshire, and Ewelme, Oxfordshire, to say nothing of chapels set apart for the tombs of individual families, as those of the Beauchamps at Warwick, and the De la Poles at Wingfield.

Happily, this monumental craft was by no means killed by the Reformation. It flourished for fully three centuries longer, though it is only recently that the later productions have been appreciated as they deserve. Work occurs by such renowned sculptors as Nicholas Stone, Roubiliac, Rysbrack, Bacon and Flaxman. During these centuries, the tombs of squires and local notabilities were often on an astonishingly ambitious scale (114) —and if their vastness and ostentation were sometimes excessive, they remain treasuries of contemporary sculpture, ornament, costume, heraldry, and lettering. The two latter crafts were likewise well displayed in the crested wall-tablets and restrained pavement slabs of the Late Renaissance.

Monumental brasses remain in great numbers, usually fixed to the floor, but occasionally considered sufficiently important to be displayed on tomb-slabs, as at Higham Ferrers and Ewelme. They appeared first in this country towards the end of the thirteenth century, and remained in vogue until the close of the fifteenth, London being the chief centre for their manufacture. While their precise detail is extraordinarily interesting to the student, they never attained in England the delicate

o

perfection to be found in Flanders and other parts of the Continent at this time.

WALL PAINTINGS

Of the schemes of colour decoration that once covered the interiors of most medieval churches practically nothing remains; they have either been obliterated by a coat of Reformation whitewash or torn down at a later date with the old plaster covering of the walls. At the same time, sufficient fragments remain, carefully catalogued and copied by modern scholars, to provide a fairly comprehensive idea of the characteristics of the mural painting at each phase.

The work was executed in distemper, and varied from simple diaperings in one or several colours to quite extensive figure-pieces and scripture scenes. The style of rendering paralleled that of the illuminated miniatures; and the effect must have been rather akin to one of these projected on the wall by a magic lantern in simple colours. Of the twelfth century, mention may be made of the range of the Apostles and the glories of heaven in the little Norman church at Kempley in Gloucestershire, the restored apse decoration, with its central figure of Christ in Glory, at Copford in Essex, and the fine roundels of New Testament scenes at Brook in Kent. Of the thirteenth, fairly complete Gospel series survive at West Chiltington in Sussex, Winterbourne Dauntsey in Wiltshire, and Easby in Yorkshire (the parish church), and of the fourteenth are the remarkable scenes in the Life of the Virgin, and Last Supper, recently recovered from under the whitewash at Croughton in Northamptonshire, and the Saints at Chalgrove and Shorthampton, Oxfordshire. With the fifteenth century, a strain of realism and a first conscious effort at pictorial composition in the Western sense began to modify the strict conventionalism of the earlier centuries. The finest work of this period, perhaps, survives in the lower panels of screens in East Anglia and Devon, already touched upon, but mention must also be made of the extensive series of wall paintings at Pickering in Yorkshire, and those of Breage in Cornwall, where there is a remarkable "Christ of the Trades," surrounded by tools and implements (116).

The two most conspicuous subjects in these decorative schemes, that have survived in the largest numbers, are the figures of St. Christopher with the Child on his shoulder, which generally faced the main entrance to the nave on the north wall, as at Breage in Cornwall (116), and, vast in size, at Shorwell in the Isle of Wight; and the Doom. The latter covered most of the wall area over the chancel arch, and represented in vivid and often grotesque detail the separation of the faithful from the sinners at the Last Judgment, and the subsequent torments of the damned. One of the finest, very Romanesque in feeling, is the twelfth-century work at Chaldon in Surrey, with its ladder connecting Heaven and Hell. Fifteenth-century Doom-paintings in fair preservation can be seen at Long Coombe in Oxfordshire and Wenhaston in Suffolk, the latter painted on boards; but the restored example at St. Thomas's at Salisbury is largest and grandest of all (115). There are interesting seventeenth-century texts in strapwork frames as at Terrington St. Clement, Norfolk, and little Partrishow in the Breconshire Black Mountains.

STAINED GLASS

Here again, in spite of the vicissitudes of later Church history, it is surprising how much medieval work can be catalogued among the parish churches, though much of this, of course, is fragmentary or restored. What remains can be classified into the four main divisions of Romanesque and early, middle, and late Gothic. Of the former, so far as parish churches are concerned, the fragments are so insignificant as to be scarcely worth mentioning, but of thirteenth-century work a fair amount remains, generally treated with figures in deep-toned medallions surrounded either by the branching scrollwork of the favourite Jesse tree, as at Westwell in Kent, or by a pale and very beautiful *grisaille* diapering, as at Chartham in the same county, Chetwode in Buckinghamshire and Stanton Harcourt in Oxfordshire. With the fourteenth century, the medallion arrangement was largely superseded by a more realistic figurework, surmounted for the first time by delicately painted canopies deriving from the pinnacled stone-work of the period, as at Stanford-on-Avon and Aldwinckle St. Peter in Northamptonshire. There was now a perceptible lightening of the wine-dark tints of the earlier work, and a widening of the colour range. It was not until the fifteenth century, however, that the old standard *pot-metal* colours, with their brown-painted detail, were immensely enriched, particularly in canopies, by the innovation of painting on the glass with the famous *silver stain*, which, when fired, produced an exuberant variety of light tints ranging from lemon to rich orange. This late medieval glass is of all, perhaps, the most beautiful, and naturally enough is to be seen in the largest quantities in the parish churches, as, in particular beauty, at Almondbury in West Yorkshire, Winscomb in Somerset and St. Neot's, Cornwall.

The system of quarries, or lozenge-shaped panes for individual devices, and the popularity of heraldic designs, were the most individual characteristics of this fifteenth-century glass. With the enlargement of windows at this time the glass-painter's art achieved a new importance, and it is fortunate that at least a few churches remain in which we can appreciate, almost intact, the lovely effects of colour and lighting that resulted. Among them, mention should certainly be made of the parish churches of the City of York—always an important centre for stained glass—particularly All Saints, North Street; the church of Fairford in Gloucestershire, where the entire original glazing has been retained; and St. Lawrence at Ludlow, with its magnificent series of Apostles and palmers in St. John's Chapel. Renaissance glass occasionally occurs.

WINCHCOMBE, GLOUCESTERSHIRE

Drawn by W. Curtis Green, R.A.

114   ELMLEY CASTLE, WORCESTERSHIRE :
The Coventry Monument (late Seventeenth Century) ;
refused admission to Croome Church

113   ST. MARK'S CHAPEL, BRISTOL: A
late-Medieval Tomb

115 ST. THOMAS OF CANTERBURY, SALISBURY: "Doom"
Painting over the Chancel Arch

116 BREAGE, CORNWALL: Wall-painting of St. Christopher,
and "Christ of the Trades"

RESTORED WALL-PAINTINGS

117 SOMERLEYTON, SUFFOLK : Screen Paintings (East Anglian type)

118 WOLBOROUGH, DEVON : Screen Paintings (West Country type)

119 CHESHAM, BUCKINGHAMSHIRE : The Needle Spire of
the Home Counties

CHAPTER FIVE

Local Varieties in Parish Church Design

AN attractive and profitable field of study, still largely unexplored, is afforded by the endeavour to determine regional characteristics in parish church-building and to ascertain if they are sufficiently distinctive to form definite local schools of design. The subject has never been adequately studied or definitely established; nevertheless sufficient material is available as a basis for further inquiry, and the present chapter, partial and tentative as it must inevitably be, may possibly serve as a fingerpost to point the way to a more detailed scheme of comparison.

The navigator in these little charted seas is sure to be faced with cross-currents, deceptive eddies and half-tide rocks; nevertheless there are outstanding landmarks on which it is possible to take bearings. Imagine, for instance, so individual a district product as a Norfolk flint church set down at the foot of the Mendips among the fifteenth-century works of Somerset, a typical Cornish building ranged with the Lincolnshire Fenland churches, or a homely Sussex hamlet fabric placed side by side with the parish buildings of Derbyshire. Put a Dorset church down in Kent, a Hampshire building in the Northumbrian Fells, or even move one from the Wiltshire limestone belt into the chalk or clay regions of the same county. The contrast between all these varieties is definite, sometimes striking, and because all this was largely hid from the eyes of students and architects of the nineteenth century, they could set down a replica of a Northamptonshire thirteenth-century church, complete with broach spire and clerestory, in an alien district where it could never be anything but an incongruous anomaly. If this inappropriateness is harsh and jarring in new churches, it produces, in Professor Prior's considered judgment, effects still more disastrous in restoration:

It has been the iniquity of revival Gothic that it has laid its cuckoo egg in the nests of old English beauty. In an interest alien to the native beauty have been imported into Kent the Northamptonshire spire, and the Norfolk flint-panelling into Devonshire.

One of the first to touch on the subject was that able observer, the late George Gilbert Scott (the younger) who wrote in 1881 : [1]

[1] *Essay on the History of English Church Architecture.*

It is curious to observe the mannerisms, so to speak, of different districts. No one could mistake a Somerset church for an East Anglian, or a Yorkshire building for one in the Midlands. Each county has its own peculiar architectural character, known to every student of our ancient architecture, while of certain buildings one says, almost instinctively, this and that were designed by the same men. In Northamptonshire almost every steeple has a stone spire; in the adjacent county of Buckingham there are, I believe, but three ancient spires, and of these two are on the border of Northants. It is quite striking in driving from the one county into the other to observe the abrupt change in the general design of the village churches, which is determined by the crossing of some nameless brooklet.

Probably the mapping out of local divergencies and mannerisms has never been undertaken seriously or on a large scale in some century and a half of ecclesiology, because the attention of Gothic revivalists was concentrated to a great extent on the chronology of features and details, with a virtual unconsciousness of comparative design: they could not see the trees for the leaves, much less comprehend the woods.

Professor Prior, though principally concerned with the greater churches, realised the interest of parish church styles, and, while sketching out on broad lines the historical basis of local divergencies,[1] urged the value of detailed research in analysis and mapping out:

It is a pity that archaeological attention was in the first fervour of the Gothic revival so much directed to the details of parish churches in the critical spirit of appreciation and depreciation rather than in that of tabulation. . . . Much might yet be done by a systematic and discriminating survey of our churches, to separate the various mason-crafts of the English quarry centres, lay out their areas, and particularly to show their influence on the great tides of central style. . . . In the parish church art, which gave the soul as it made up the bulk, of Perpendicular Gothic, batches of churches separate themselves as distinctive. Moreover, this wide and interesting field has been but little explored. If such prominent differences as that of the church-building of Norfolk from that of Somerset, or that of the Yorkshire fifteenth century from the Devonshire has been recognised, there remain some score of others waiting to be characterised. The investigation of Gothic style has been most largely of its detail, but only up to 1400 was there that continual progress in this easily recognised attribute to justify the exclusive attention given to this side of the story. The advance of Perpendicular was no longer conditioned by detail, which remained prac-

---

[1] *History of Gothic Art in England*, pp. 252, 366, 446.

tically the same over a period of nearly 150 years. In the history of our latest Gothic the tale had still a different telling in every country-side; for the artist had his local audience, and played up to their humours.

It is not easy to define how different regional schools of design originated; no doubt the local masons worked out mannerisms in general design, features and details which in the course of years coalesced and hardened into a tradition. But other factors which acted as influences were the character, great or little, of the local materials, their abundance, variety and adaptability, the extent of water transport available to bring good stone easily from a distance, the density of settle-ment, and the industrial development or stagnation of a district. The wool industry of the Cotswolds and East Anglia, the prosperity of Somerset, the mining of Cornwall, all led to the production of great groups of churches which showed marked regional characteristics. Not least was that root-tendency in human nature, local rivalry—communities would vie with each other in the height of their towers, the peal of their bells, the richness of their screenwork, all of definitely local type.

It may be well to review characteristic buildings of one or two of the most strongly marked of these regional varieties. If we consider side by side a typical Devon or Cornish church (139, 142) and a Fenland limestone building (121) nothing could appear more divergent. There is the severe fifteenth-century building of the West, with its continuous line of long low roofs, nave and aisles ending in two or three gables, without clerestory, but with a row of great Perpen-dicular windows. At the west is a sturdy porch, four square, with deeply recessed battlements, and the whole is sur-mounted by a strong, tall, pinnacled tower (76), eloquent in its stern simplicity of the material of its construction. Then contrast with this the oolite church of the Fens, where work of the thirteenth and fourteenth centuries predominates. There is a well-defined clerestory, the chancel projects eastward clear of the shorter aisle-chapels, the wide porch is gabled and the tall tower is crowned with a lofty spire. The masonry is equally interesting to compare. The Cornish church has rough granite blocks, while in Devonshire we find as well fairly narrow courses of slaty stone, both distinct from the finished ashlar of the oolite. Within, the difference is of equal interest. In the South-Western building the characteristic fifteenth-century piers are surmounted by three plastered barrel vaults (140), an elaborately carved screen (if it has not disappeared) stretches continuously across nave and aisles from wall to wall (31), and there are richly carved late bench ends. The Fenland church does not possess these special features, though screen and bench ends are of fine design if extant.

Another interesting comparison is between a northern church (149) and an example from Sussex (122). There are many varieties of churches in the great expanse of Yorkshire, so that a summing up of their design is not easy; some indications are given later (p. 112). Many of the churches of the South-Eastern Yorkshire plain are splendid buildings, which vie in design and workmanship with any in England. The churches of the uplands have a certain stamp not easy to define; they are not wanting in dignity or defined character, but there is often a certain air of austere reserve about them, as about their surroundings, in marked contrast to the homely character of the less ambitious churches of Sussex. In the latter the long sloping roofs are suggestive of the sweeping covering of the tiled cottages, and the low tower is crowned with a tiled cap or small perky shingled spire. The scanty local materials are applied with resourcefulness to produce a result that charms by its very fortuitousness, and is in harmony with the peaceful friendly countryside, where hill and woodland, meadow, stream and homestead blend into the most essentially English of landscapes.

The East Anglian is another well-marked type, consistently worked out and well adapted to its materials, of which the qualities are applied with the utmost skill. This church with its massive tower of flint (72), often with but slight battlements or pinnacles, and no prominent stair-turret, its long lantern-like clerestory and high-pitched roofs over nave and chancel, is a splendid monument of craftsmanship. The effect, with its flushwork porch and panelling as at Eye (144), is one of impressive stateliness. The interior usually has plain octagonal piers and capitals, a rich hammerbeam roof, possibly carved or painted screen, and fine benches.

But like other truths, such as the expression of racial qualities in buildings, the differentiation of these varieties can be stressed too strongly, and if followed too far the way will peter out in shallows and quicksands. If the conditions of English medieval building are generally recalled, it will not be found surprising that in many parts there are humble buildings of so ordinary a type that they are devoid of any regional characteristic, and might have been put up in almost any country district. This is specially the case with neighbourhoods devoid of any vigorous expansion or rebuilding of the

120 LELANT, CORN-
WALL : The Austerity
of the Far West, in a
typical setting

121 HECKINGTON,
LINCOLNSHIRE: The
Summit of Curvilinear
achievement in the East-
ern Marshlands

122 LITLINGTON, SUSSEX: The "Small Stoneless" Type
of the South-east

123 HARESCOMBE, GLOUCESTERSHIRE: A Hamlet Church
of "Small Stone" Type

124 MERSTHAM, SURREY

125 KNEBWORTH, HERTFORDSHIRE

VILLAGE CHURCHES OF THE HOME COUNTIES

127 SANDON

126 BLACKMORE

ESSEX INDIVIDUALITY IN TIMBER AND BRICK

parochial fabrics in later medieval times. With its low tower, or shingled spirelet, narrow aisles, small porch and unchapel'd chancel, such a building would require an expert geological examination of its detail or masonry before its provenance could be definitely confirmed. Frequently only a proportion, great or small, of the churches of any given county display a well-marked local character, as in Lincolnshire, where the splendid works of middle or late medieval craftsmanship are scattered among ordinary, indeed even nondescript or mean, buildings. In some parts, especially in Somerset, Devon and Cornwall, almost every fabric was molded into a definite regional shape; in others it must be acknowledged that the masterpieces for which a neighbourhood is famous are comparatively few, and are, as it were, superimposed on the background of average ordinary material, like first magnitude stars scintillating against an array of faint lesser lights. Some buildings are markedly individual rather than regional, e.g. the elaborate surface carving at Launceston. Again, the distribution of well-marked manners of building over whole counties, especially in the South-West, which usually postulate general rebuilding, mostly in the fifteenth century, must be sharply differentiated from the group occurrence of particular methods of plan or construction, also found elsewhere. An instance of this is the central tower transeptal type found in Wiltshire, such as Potterne and Amesbury, with examples right through at the foot of the chalk escarpment to beyond the Chilterns, such as Chesham (119), Ivinghoe and Foulmire (*alias* Fowlmere).

The approximate local varieties may, it is suggested, be roughly classified as follows:

1. The *"Small Stone"* *type of church*, occurring quite generally in stone-producing districts, or where a supply of stone is readily available. Not a very well-defined variety, more of a "background" type. Pretty widely distributed.

2. The *"Small Stoneless"* *type*, prevalent throughout districts producing no stone, especially in the South-East of England, with its special outliers of *Kent* and *Essex*.

3. The *"Limestone Belt"* *types*, running north-east from Gloucestershire to Lincolnshire, with an outlier of magnesian limestone in South-Eastern Yorkshire; more specialised at its southern end, and changing like a banded spectrum by way of the normal Oxfordshire church and the work of Northamptonshire and its adjacent counties to the well-defined varieties of the Fenlands.

Q

4. *The South-Western types,* divided into three varieties: Somerset, Devon and Cornwall, each more specialised in design and materials with the further westerly position.

5. *The East Anglian type,* abundant in Norfolk and Suffolk, a finished product in material and craftsmanship.

6. *The Churches of the Midlands:* (a) *Northern,* (b) *Western.* (*a*) Nottinghamshire, Derbyshire, Leicestershire, Staffordshire. A fairly homogeneous division in itself, though less distinctive than the Northamptonshire group, with which it has some relationship. (*b*) Warwickshire, Worcestershire and the four Welsh Border counties, having no very special characteristics but some local peculiarities, like the use of half timber-work for belfries or even fabrics.

7. *The Churches of the North,* a vast unclassified area over which no uniformity prevails, generally a kind of austere small stone type with outstanding larger examples, though there is a certain relationship in the general effect of the design of many examples, with district peculiarities as in No. 6.

These types will be discussed more fully later in the chapter. There are obvious drawbacks in this or any other scheme; the limitations in attempting to determine local differences are manifold and confront the student early in the subject.

The State has recognised the importance of records of historic buildings in view of war destruction and damage by the creation of the National Buildings Record as a section of the Ministry of Works and Buildings. Under the direction of Mr. W. H. Godfrey, F.S.A., F.R.I.B.A., it is now collecting and collating data of all kinds which will form an invaluable record. Material is also being collected, exclusively for churches, under the auspices of the Central Council for the Care of Churches, in connection with the Church of England Central Council of Diocesan Advisory Committees, organised by Dr. E. C. Eeles, O.B.E. The Courtauld Institute of Art has also got together an extensive series of church photographs. The vast corpus of drawings by J. C. Buckler of about 1830 is invaluable—the County series of some fifty volumes in the British Museum and the complete surveys of Hertfordshire, now in the St. Albans Museum, and Wiltshire, in the Devizes Museum. In both writing and illustration the parish church has received in general the piecemeal and fragmentary treatment meted out to the poor relation, due to the unrelenting preoccupation of nearly everyone with the greater churches, or with parts and detail.

Naturally any attempt at such a classification cannot consent to be pegged down to the arbitrary divisions of the

128   PEMBRIDGE, HEREFORDSHIRE : The detached Belfry

129   NEW ROMNEY, KENT : Showing the typical " Three-Gable "
arrangement of this County

130 EAST HARLING, NORFOLK : A stately East Anglian design

131 BOUGHTON ALUPH, KENT : An Example of unusual Planning

counties; indeed, local varieties are not even entirely coterminous with, though much influenced by, the geological distribution. Nevertheless, there are cases, as in the South-West,
where the counties do express roughly the extent of a type,
and certainly their names must be retained as convenient units
for discussion; as flag labels, to quote the tag of the patent
medicines, there is no substitute.

Little or nothing can be discerned of regional variety in
Anglo-Norman building;—the style of the conquerors,
whether austere or exuberant, was, in their mighty outburst,
of a strong uniformity, like the buildings of those greater
colonisers, the Romans themselves. The tall cylinders of West
Country Romanesque piers in the larger churches scarcely
affect parish design, though not without possible later influence. In later medieval times the greater town churches
also form an exception; the means to command a fine grade
of craftsmanship, possibly from a distance or from varied
sources, causes them to be less strongly stamped with the
characteristics of the district.

To run cursorily over the suggested tentative divisions:

1. *The Small Stone Type.*—Churches which might be
described as of the "small stone" variety occur almost everywhere that some sort of stone could be easily procured: in
remote or backward districts, poor in resources or inferior in
materials, it may be the prevailing or almost universal sort of
building, and even in parts famous for fine churches you
may in small hamlets not infrequently meet the humble village
fabric with low tower or stone bellcote, as at Harescombe (123),
showing little local variation from the Lincolnshire Wolds to
the Welsh Border hills, or from the Westmorland fells to the
Dorset coast. On account of its wide and sporadic distribution
it would be difficult to describe any series of examples in a
concise way, but as there is little that is distinctive, it is un-
necessary to do so. This type can also be contrasted with the
"small stoneless," *vide* pp. 98–101. It will generally be found that
the average standard of window tracery in village churches is
higher in districts where the churches are of the small stone
type than in stoneless neighbourhoods where the builders
often had recourse to more or less makeshift expedients; the
same would apply to capitals and piers in aisled examples, the
stone districts being superior to the frequently rude and
clumsy work of districts which had to rely on odd imported
or inferior stone.

These unpretentious products of a simple village masoncraft often make a definite appeal by their sterling sincerity,

appropriateness, and good proportions. Generally built and roofed entirely of local materials, with square-headed windows, plain porch and low tower or western gable bellcote, such hamlet churches as Yelford and Clanfield in Oxfordshire, Little Washbourne or Saintbury in the Cotswolds or Manton in Rutland, can hold their own in quiet dignity with more ambitious and pretentious structures.

2. *The Small Church of Stoneless Districts.*—Next is considered a form of church found in a group of South-Eastern counties which were practically stoneless or possessed of distinctly inferior kinds. In this division the counties of Bedford, Buckingham, Berkshire, Middlesex, Hertford and Essex, may be included, as well as Surrey, Sussex, Hampshire, and to some extent Wiltshire and South Oxfordshire. On each side of the Thames estuary, Essex and Kent produced rather more outstanding varieties, which will be considered later in the section. All these counties resorted to the use of timber, but in different degrees, and all made some use of flint. There is little that is very marked about the character of these churches, mostly small structures serving humble villages. Clerestories do not often occur except in the buildings of the country towns, and the aisles are built either with flat roofs from the top of the nave wall, or else the slope of the nave roof is continued in one long sweep over the aisle, as at Bury and Amberley. The unaisled transeptal form with low central tower is sometimes seen in Surrey (Chipstead) and Hampshire (Breamore). In Sussex much Transitional building is found, and Norman and thirteenth-century work is common.

The small village church has in this area the characteristic little wooden belfry or bellcote over the west gable, with a shingled spirelet, blunt or slender. Of this there are abundant examples in the South-Eastern group; in Surrey (Elstead, Crowhurst), Kent (Fawkham, Dymchurch), Sussex (Heyshott, Litlington (122)), and Tangmere, etc. It should be understood that no contrivance of this kind was usually resorted to where stone could fairly readily be obtained, even for the smallest churches, though wooden bellcotes are frequent in timber-traditioned parts, like Shropshire. Except for its type of bellcote, the character of its walling, and usually more finish in the windows and doors there is no striking difference between the smaller churches in either stone or stoneless districts. Indeed, there is often a considerable resemblance, if we compare such buildings as Cocking in Sussex and Sarnesfield in Herefordshire.

Bedfordshire is less destitute of stone than the rest of this group. In some parts flint, clunch and Silsoe sandstone are used in walling. The limestone belt churches of the North of the county receive mention in that division. The stone chiefly used is from Totternhoe in the South; it is a soft stone adapted for internal work, but weathers badly. The prevailing form is chancel, aisled nave and western tower, but occasionally the cruciform kind with central tower occurs on the Cambridgeshire border. There are a few stone spires.

In *Buckinghamshire* much of the walling is rough rubble under plaster or rough-cast; in the North the occurrence of limestone is coterminous with superior construction and occasional richness of detail. There are only two old stone spires, at Olney (83) and Hanslope, but a few small ones are of lead-covered timber.

In *Berkshire* good building material is scanty. The towers are mostly low and plain; in some smaller churches there is a wooden belfry on timber framing as at Old Didcot. In the North-West, stone is more generally used, sometimes sarsen from the Downs. There is a string of interesting churches just north of the Downs; at West Shefford and Welford are round flint Norman towers, but the only old stone spires occur at St. Helen's Abingdon, Shottesbrooke and Shellingford.

In *Middlesex* a large proportion of the churches have been rebuilt on poor lines to accommodate increasing populations. Absence of building stone and difficulties of carriage, save by the Thames, caused most walls to be built of rubble, untrimmed flints and pudding stone, with dressings of clunch from Hertfordshire and Surrey. Good Ketton stone is used occasionally for windows and doorways. At Hayes, Hillingdon and Ruislip the walls are faced with trimmed black flints.

In the eastern part of *Hertfordshire* flints abound; and there is no stone save chalk. In the North-West, the churches closely resemble those of Bedfordshire, the material coming from the Totternhoe quarries. The lead covered timber spire of Hemel Hempstead is a fine lofty example of the fourteenth century; and there is another at Stevenage. A characteristic feature is the small tapering *flèche* or leaded spirelet on the towers, sometimes derisively termed "extinguishers" or "Hertfordshire needles"; of this good examples occur at Chesham and Knebworth (119, 125). In the chalk uplands of Wiltshire and the Chiltern hills of South Oxfordshire the churches are of unpretentious "small stoneless" kind, often with flint walling.

The four South-Eastern counties of *Surrey, Sussex, Kent,* and *Hampshire* constitute a sub-division where the local stones were inferior and scanty, and water carriage, save on the coast, indifferent or wanting. The two counties of the old diocese of Winchester, Hampshire and Surrey, are of the small stoneless type, in the main timber-steepled; Sussex also takes its place in this category, but Kent stands somewhat by itself, and is regarded as a specialised outlier.

Hampshire has in addition a few timber towers (Hurstbourne Tarrant), some shingled like their spires, and a selection of wooden western porches, as at Warblington and Sherborne. The twin naves in some of the self-contained little group of the Isle of Wight have already been mentioned (p. 33).

Amidst the welter of rebuilding and restoration to which the once primitive hamlet churches of Surrey have been subjected it is difficult to extract much that is distinctive, but Thursley and Crowhurst are quite pleasant small stoneless buildings with their graceful spirelets, and Oxted is of the stumpy western towered cruciform variety. Great Bookham (48) is interesting and unspoilt, though its belfry recalls Essex, just as that of Wotton smacks of the Welsh Border. Merstham (124) and Shere are more pretentious—the latter is a remarkably attractive village church—but their gabled chapels and spires are reminiscent of Kent.

Sussex presents a somewhat heterogeneous assortment of buildings, many of them small and primitive, and hence rather attractive for study. They occur with and without clerestories, having often low or medium-high towers, battlemented or surmounted by tall (Bury, Heathfield) or stumpy (Dallington, Newhaven) shingled timber spires of the "chamfered broach" sort. There are many timber spirelets, dropping by degrees into the simple bellcotes of such churches as Heyshott, Wilmington, and elsewhere, or the tiny one-bell top, as at Coombes. Two really typical Sussex features, by no means confined to the county, are, as already mentioned, the continuous slope of roof over nave and aisle, well shown at Climping and Yapton—this is closely paralleled in cottage building; and the blunt pyramidal form of tower covering—shown at Cocking, Clymping, and other places. It is sometimes called "the Sussex cap," and is probably a survival of the customary form of tower termination in Norman times.

If the medieval church builders of *Essex* seldom produced a very outstanding or individual type of design, except in their belfries, they are distinguished for the able and effective use of brick and timber to counteract the entire absence of good building stone. It is curious that the county stands apart ecclesiologically from its two northern neighbours, the ancient

132 CHIPPING CAMPDEN INTERIOR

133 THORNBURY TOWER

THE FIFTEENTH CENTURY IN GLOUCESTERSHIRE

134 WARBOYS, HUNTINGDONSHIRE: A Broach Spire on the edge of the Stone Belt

kingdom of East Anglia, just as it had little share in their industrial development. If flint is used it is as plain walling, not "flushwork," and only a few round towers have crossed the border. But the late medieval craftsmen of Essex set as high a standard in their churches as in the domestic buildings in which their county is still so rich. In brick only brief mention can be made of a few outstanding examples, such as the diapered towers of Sandon (127) and Ingatestone, the porch of Feering, the porch and clerestory of Great Baddow, and windows at Sandon and Feering. All these show an understanding and sympathetic handling of the material. St. Osyth has a fine late arcade entirely of brick; at Shenfield the fifteenth-century arcade is entirely of timber, and individual timber arches are of occasional occurrence. But the belfries, Essex's most original contribution, are of quite varied design and often take the form of diminishing stages, as at Blackmore (126), Thundersley, and, on the plan of a Greek cross, at West Hanningfield.

Though the churches of *Kent* form a decidedly mixed collection, there are well-marked local features. Chief is the general absence of clerestories, forming a curious parallel with the other peninsula at the south-western end of England. The method of putting nave and aisles under separate gables results in a number of cases, such as Lynsted and New Romney (129), in the "three gable" east end, so characteristic of Cornwall. But more frequent is the "two gable" termination of chancel and one chantry chapel, such as Boughton Aluph (131), the latter often stopping short of the full length of the former, as at Rolvenden. The tall severe tower of Kentish ragstone is also characteristic, its angle stair turret rising well above the battlements, as at Newington, Charing, Maidstone All Saints, etc. But as elsewhere there are medium or low towers, often with stumpy "timber broach" spires, as at Westerham and Lynsted, churches which may be selected as examples of very individual Kentish design. The type of Decorated tracery individual to the county is well seen at Chartham and elsewhere.

3. *The Churches of the Limestone Belt.* The great oolite belt, running from the Bristol Channel to the Humber, naturally produced many fine examples of masoncraft throughout its length. As might be expected, however, there is no prevailing type of church—the design shades like the rainbow from Gloucestershire through Oxfordshire and Northamptonshire to the Lincolnshire Fenlands, and any classification is rather in the nature of scattered groups. Somerset, Dorset and

Wiltshire with its limestone section are best reckoned with the South-West, and Derbyshire, Nottinghamshire, Leicestershire and Staffordshire, though having some relationship to Northamptonshire and its neighbours, are perhaps more conveniently set apart in a North Midland group.

In *Gloucestershire* there are some fine towers, as Yate and Thornbury (133), on the west towards Somerset, but a distinctive feature of the slender stone spires which occasionally occur is a roll molding at the angles (Slimbridge); if with broaches these are very stumpy, as at Bisley, and occasionally pinnacled (Mickleton). The Cotswold churches somewhat resemble the normal Oxfordshire type; in many smaller villages they are unaisled, and some have stone bellcotes. The Cotswold wool fabrics form a splendid group of stately slender Perpendicular—Cirencester (47), Northleach, Winchcombe (p. 90) and Chipping Campden (132); most have a large window over the chancel arch, a feature also found at Chipping Norton. *Oxfordshire* has a good series of quite normal medium-sized churches, and the occurrence of big central-towered buildings with typical pinnacled-broach spires calls for special mention—e.g. Witney and Bampton; Burford with a parapet spire is also a complex agglomeration of aisles and chapels. A type of tall rectangular late clerestory window with long hood molds is individual, as at Great Tew, and South Newington; also at Long Compton in Warwickshire.

With *Northamptonshire*, that Mecca of the Victorian ecclesiologists, must be grouped North Bedfordshire and North Buckinghamshire, Cambridgeshire, Rutland and Huntingdonshire, whose glorious fabrics have been unaccountably ignored or neglected. It is not too much to say that these two latter counties, the smallest in England, have the highest proportion of fine churches in the land, but no adequate review of their riches is possible here. The special feature of the fame of this section is of course the broach spire, as at Raunds, Ketton (85), Warboys (134), Spaldwick, Pickworth (135), among many; but there are fine parapeted spires—Oundle (7), Kettering, Tilbrook; and great towers—St. Neots, Connington, Titchmarsh, Whiston, Aldwinkle All Saints, etc. The spire with big broaches is indigenous towards the northerly part of the limestone belt—the Gloucestershire type is entirely different, as mentioned above. The pinnacled broach Oxfordshire group is also distinct (*v. supra*); and of this Olney (83), Adderbury, and King's Sutton, rich with double pinnacles, are about the most Northern instances. The broach examples range from the stumpy caps of Lyddington and Upper Hambleton

136 UPPER HAMBLETON, RUTLAND

135 PICKWORTH, LINCOLNSHIRE

BROACH SPIRES OF THE STONE BELT

137 WOODFORD, NORTHAMPTONSHIRE : Structural Evolution
through the Twelfth and Thirteenth Centuries

138 PUDDLETOWN, DORSET : A delightful village Interior,
untouched by the Restorer

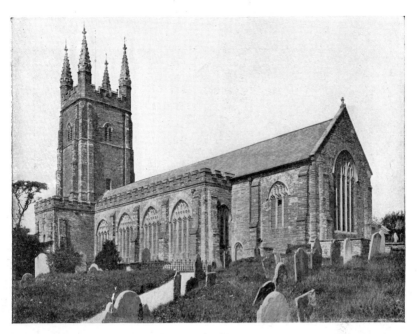

139 WEST ALVINGTON, DEVON: The County type at its best

140 LAUNCESTON, CORNWALL: A typical Non-Clerestoreyed
Interior of the South-west, with plastered Wagon Roofs

141 HUISH EPISCOPI, SOMERSET: One of the loveliest Perpendicular Towers of this County, in a typical Setting

(136) to the towering height of Ketton (85), Keystone, or those mentioned in Chap. IV (p. 69). The chamfered broach derived from timber is seen in such churches as Denford and Etton in Northamptonshire and Bythorn in Huntingdonshire. Equally fine broach spires are found in the North Midland group in Leicestershire, e.g. at Ab-Kettleby and Kirby Bellairs. But there a shorter type is also found, as at Shepsted, which occurs also in Nottinghamshire, as at Holme, and in Derbyshire (Hope). Yet throughout this group there are spires with lantern storeys—Exton, Wilby, etc.; and later parapet spires are also prevalent—Whittlesea, Heckington, Moulton, the Bottesfords. This type predominates further North in Derbyshire, Staffordshire and on to the Yorkshire Wolds—Repton, Chilmorton, etc. The individual feature of Northamptonshire proper is the use of the orange-brown ironstone with the white to produce a particoloured effect, as at Finedon (p. 62), Woodford (137) and elsewhere in the Nene Valley. But if, as must be confessed, the low thirteenth-century arcades of Higham Ferrers (p. 62), the Aldwinckles and many other places are stunted in effect, there is Perpendicular lightness and grace at Whiston (p. 62), Lowick and Fotheringay (p. 62). The smaller *Rutland* churches affect a stone bellcote, usually with two openings, as at Manton, Little Casterton, etc. In Southern *Lincolnshire* the broach spires are even more overwhelming in such mighty works as Ewerby and Threckingham, with crocketed examples such as Walcot. Apart from these masterpieces, consider the dignity of such ordinary village churches as Ryhall near Stamford and Great Ponton near Grantham. But the rich and delicate grace of Lincolnshire Curvilinear work has possibly not yet been fully appreciated, in such buildings as Heckington (121), Boston (4), Holbeach, Swaton and Aunsby. There are other splendid churches, often built of Barnack stone brought along the watercourses, but in the North part of the county are many decent ordinary medium-sized churches, with some undistinguished and even poor examples with squat towers. The limestone Fenland buildings over or near the Norfolk border (29, 34, 37) are, in spite of their material, definitely East Anglian in type. *Cambridgeshire* is very mixed in its church types, with some East Anglian outliers and flint buildings by the chalk, but its limestone Fenland fabrics, such as Leverington and Whittlesea, are as splendid as any.

4. *The Churches of the South-West.*—Dorset may be considered as including one end of the oolite belt, while Wiltshire has churches as mixed as its geological formations, and Somerset

R

with its glorious towers shades into the well-marked Devon style, of which Cornwall is a more extreme form.

In *Wiltshire* there are "small stoneless" churches of flint on and around the chalk downs, with low towers or timber bellcotes, like Boscombe and George Herbert's Bemerton. The "small stone" structures of the oolite band have often a local kind of stone bellcote, partly curved. This county sees the dying out of the stone spire, and Pirton and Wanborough have both western towers and central spires. If many of the spacious and fine churches are not specially striking in local character, buildings such as Steeple Ashton, Devizes St. Mary and Avebury, with their well-marked clerestories, profuse battlements and pinnacles and well-proportioned towers, are a distinctive product, and a gracious one at that. *Dorset* churches are of a good standard, without any remarkable qualities. The rather plain towers are of many heights and sizes, but have typically a bold octagonal stair turret projecting well above the roof. It is very characteristic of the county for the turret to be itself battlemented and sometimes pinnacled (p. 22), though this is not universal. There are many unaisled village fabrics; of the aisled examples some are clerestoried, but most typically the aisle springs from the nave wall plate and is battlemented throughout, with often a square battlemented porch. The aisle usually stops to leave clear the last bay of the chancel; the "two gable" arrangement does not occur.

If the chief glory of *Somerset* churches is their towers, (3, 141), their splendid screens also call for notice, though there is no space here to review their remarkable variety of design. The towers, the finest achievement of fifteenth-century masoncraft, have a certain unity, with all their difference in form, feature and detail. They rise sheer, almost without batter, and the stair turret is not usually unduly emphasised. The number of windows differs, with one, two or three in the topmost storey; there is usually a large window on the ground storey, dwarfing the west doorway. Their straight upstanding lines are scarcely affected by the pair of buttresses each side of every angle, generally finishing with a pinnacle at the summit. There is no opportunity here to discuss methods of their classification, based on their group-occurrence and their fenestration. At the briefest of glances, some are sturdy, such as Kingston or Staple Fitzpaine; some slender, such as Publow, Winford or Cheddar; others seem to achieve both height and massiveness, as Bishop's Lydeard and Huish Episcopi (141). There are towers of grave simplicity like Chew

142　ST. NEOTS, CORNWALL : The Severity of the Far West

143 ACLE, NORFOLK: A Round Tower in East Anglian Flint, with later
Octagonal Upper Storey. The Roofing is of Thatch

Magna or Norton-sub-Hamdon, or of exuberant richness, such as North Petherton, Leigh on Mendip and St. Mary Magdalene, Taunton. Two rather divergent varieties may be mentioned; in the first the window lines run down into the next storey below, exemplified by St. Cuthbert's at Wells (38), Evercreech and Wrington (3); in the other a plain structure is surmounted by an elaborate capping of openwork parapet and pinnacle; such are Dundry and St. Stephen's, Bristol. There are, of course, exceptional designs like Ilminster, and outliers are found at Chittlehampton in Devon, Probus in Cornwall and elsewhere. The body of the church often appears insignificant in comparison with the tallness of the tower, though not so markedly as in Cornwall; they are often fine buildings with a wide spacious interior. In design they "shade" towards the west; such a building as Luccombe is practically Devonian. The chancel arch is usual, and aisled examples are about equally divided between the clerestoried and "two gable" type, though the last chancel bay usually projects clear. The tall Perpendicular aisle windows have often cusped transoms (71), and two local variations of tracery can be found. There is often an exterior rood stair turret; pierced parapets or battlements both occur and the two-storeyed porch may be gabled or square (87). Transepts occur fairly frequently, some in connection with a central tower as at Axbridge; this may be octagonal, as at Doulting (44) and Somerton, the latter transeptal in position. A word must be said of the county roofs—the graceful kingpost type of Wellow and St. Cuthbert's, Wells (49), the tiebeam of Bruton, and the rich panelling of Mark, only outdone by the minute panelled elaboration of Shepton Mallet, with some 350 divisions. The latter is of the rounded South-Western type, and some churches on the Devon border have the usual wagon-vaulted plastered roofs.

The churches of *Devon*, almost entirely fifteenth-century, are still more specialised; naturally in the third largest English county they differ considerably among themselves—towers are in unusual positions, or break out into shingled or lead spires (Barnstaple, Braunton). Transepts are fairly common; chancel arches are also occasionally found, but clerestories are excessively exceptional (Crediton). In size and finish the fabrics are also widely different; some are rich with elaborate Western craftsmanship; some small remote structures are grim without and bucolically rustic within. It is best to sketch the appearance of a typical Devon church and indicate a few customary variations. The tall western tower rises high and austere above the low roofs, generally with a huge stair turret, which is often placed rather curiously in the middle of, or partly along, one side, as at Buckland, Ashburton (76). The aisle with its two-storey porch stands out square and battle-mented (139); or possibly it may be gabled; sometimes it runs the whole length of the structure, but usually stops short of the last chancel bay. The "three gable" east end is not general. There are usually arched Perpendicular windows, but some-times the square kind is preferred. Within, the arches are plain and simple, and around Dartmoor the capitals will be of the funnel shape found worked in granite all over the South-West; with more tractable stone they can be foliated (Berry Narbor), or incorporate angel supporters (St. Petrock, Exeter) or other figures (South Molton). But if the mason has had to restrain himself, the woodworker has rioted rejoicingly. The great elaborate screen, traceried and vaulted, with serried rows of fine detail above, runs unbroken from wall to wall, while above it arch the three wagon-vaulted roofs, plastered or showing the rafters. There is a fine medieval pulpit of wood or stone, and the bench ends, plain or rich, make up an ensemble which retains much of its original medieval grace and feeling. If the *Cornish* churches constitute a still more specialised product, both in design and materials (one, indeed, of the most individual in the Kingdom (142)), they can by no means be considered as standardised. The fifteenth-century South-Western type here receives its most emphatic development, and granite greatly predominates. Clerestories and chancel arches have vanished; the towers could be ranged in a graded series from the short and stumpy (Mullion) to such heights as Linkinhorne and St. Columb Minor. The low slate roofs stretch in a continuous line as at Lelant (120), occasionally cut by a wide transept (e.g. Lan-drake). The wide low porches are usually gabled, but may be two-storeyed and square (St. Neots). The simplified granite tracery can be under three-centred arches, or may be all square (St. Buryan). At the east end there are often two gables, for one wide aisle gives the effect of twin naves. There may be three gables, but in either case the aisles may let the chancel have the last feet in projection; St. Ives manages four gables in line. In the interior the four-fold engaged shafts with funnel-like capitals hold the field with slight differences in proportion and detail; though there are occasional plain octagonal shafts and solid capitals, the arches are plainly molded. Similarly the wagon-vaulted roof is universal, whether pleasantly plastered or with rafters exposed. Most screens have disappeared, but the fine series of bench-ends, still considerable in spite of rabid nineteenth-century evictions, has already been noticed (p. 82). Such interiors as Mullion (18), and Kilkhampton (where the arcades are of exceptional height, as also at Launceston (140)), undoubtedly express in a real way the character of their rugged yet gracious land, and the genius of the race that produced them.

5. *The East Anglian Type of Norfolk and Suffolk.*—The parish churches of Norfolk and Suffolk, the counties of the old Kingdom of East Anglia, are of a very individual and out-standing type. Nevertheless, on account of their great number, and the strong contrasts in country and population, there

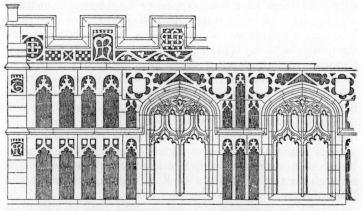

FLINT "FLUSHWORK" PANELLING ON THE CLERESTORY
OF CODDENHAM CHURCH, SUFFOLK

are enormous differences in size, design, appearance and arrangement; indeed, an ascending scale could be formed from the smallest primitive buildings to vast stately fabrics. Here English fifteenth-century building genius takes on another form: with exteriors of dressed flint, often patterned ingeniously with the thin slabs of freestone called flush-work. This is applied to clerestories, porches, plinths, tower crestings, etc., and at times includes saints' emblems and other devices. Southwold is a very rich example, as is St. Michael Coslany, Norwich; typical work is also seen at Coddenham, Laxfield, Eye (144), Earl Stonham and many other places. The clerestory is usually tall, occasionally with circular openings (Cley, Frettenham), but often with windows of any frequency up to the practically continuous ranges of Long Melford (10), Bury St. Edmunds (40) or St. Peter Mancroft, Norwich (75). Battlements or parapets are infrequent; if they occur they are often most elaborate, as at Lavenham (72), and there are pierced examples on porches (Cley, Pulham S.M.V.). Above the clerestory the nave roof is usually high pitched, e.g. East Harling (130); the Eastern church folk did not take kindly to the flattish roof, just as they discarded reluctantly Curvilinear for Perpendicular forms, using them alternatively, devising transition patterns. Roofing with reed thatching has occasionally survived (Edingthorpe, Bramfield, Hales, Acle (143)), and pantiles are sometimes found (Beeston St. Lawrence). The fine porches have already been touched upon (p. 72); and the frequent round towers have been mentioned earlier, p. 68 (51); many of these are Saxon or Norman, and they have often been later capped or heightened, sometimes with an octagonal belfry storey (Acle (143), Rickinghall Inferior). The square towers are of many shapes and heights, rising to the grandeur of Eye (144), Lavenham (72), South Repps and Cromer; though possibly such medium-sized examples as Dennington, Redenhall, Walcot and Wilby are most typical. Though many towers are without capping, a type of stepped battlement is very characteristic, as are the square traceried openings—the so-called "soundholes." The stair turrets are inconspicuous. A possibly gaunt exterior gives no clue to what is found within, where dignified austerity may be combined with such simple rich craftsmanship as has passed through the triple onslaught of Reformation, Revolution and "Restoration." Piers may be very tall octagons, or have the frequent four-engaged shafts with molded caps, and multiple arch moldings in two sections. Above may be a quite early trussed rafter roof, or the splendour of a single or double hammerbeam specimen, often studded with a carved company of the angelic host (Knapton, March (91)). There may be one of the glorious "Seven-Sacrament" fonts (as at East Dereham (89)), or a mighty font-cover like Ufford (100) or Trunch. And perhaps may also be found the wreckage of a once glorious screen, as at Bramford or Attleborough, occasionally still keeping its painted saints and apostles, as in the Broadland group of Ranworth and Ludham. Then there are fine ranges of benches, as at Fressingfield and Wiggenhall the Virgin (102) and St. Germans. South-west of Lynn the marshland folk have shown what could be done to give a limestone version of the East Anglian type: the miniature galaxy of the Terrington's (29, 37), Tilney's (34), Walpole's (17), and Wiggenhall's must be seen, for no description can possibly convey its radiance.

144 EYE, SUFFOLK: A splendidly proportioned East Anglian Tower
of the Fifteenth Century in Flint Flushwork

145   ROCKFIELD, MONMOUTHSHIRE: The long slope of the Roofs, and Belfry Design, are
typical of the Welsh Borderland

6. *The Churches of the Midlands.*

(*a*) *The North Midlands: Leicestershire, Nottinghamshire, Derbyshire, Staffordshire.*

These four counties are much akin, and their structures are built partly of a variety of limestones and partly in more friable sandstones. Naturally enough Leicestershire is influenced by its immediate neighbours, Northamptonshire and Rutland, and Nottinghamshire by Lincolnshire. All four counties make a good average showing without anything outstanding, except great late town churches, such as St. Mary's at Nottingham, Stafford and Leicester, East Retford, Market Harborough and Chesterfield, which, as might be expected, show little of local characteristics. Generally, chancels are unaisled throughout, and clerestories and aisles are fully battlemented, occasionally with a few small pinnacles; sometimes this treatment is also applied to chancels and porches, which are usually of a one-storey gabled kind. The fenestration of clerestories and aisles is almost invariably square-headed, and even the fine Decorated chancel of Tideswell has this form. The use of heavy stone slates for roofing has sometimes led to some flattening of roofs, as at Chilmorton. Spires are frequent; sometimes short broach, as at Hope, Baslow, or Hallaton; more often parapet, like Castle Donnington, Breadsall, Sawley. There is quite a good school of tower-building, usually of dignified sturdy proportions; as examples may be cited Tideswell, Elvaston, Rolleston, Longford. For typical *village* churches of good design and proportion the following may be selected, rather haphazardly, among a number of others equally worthy of mention (excluding the outstanding town examples):

Leicestershire: Stanford, Bottesford, Kirby Bellairs, Gaddesby, Kegworth.
Nottinghamshire: Leake, Weston, Beckingham, East Drayton, Babworth.
Derbyshire: Hope, Repton, Hathersage, Baslow, Tideswell, Melbourne, Norbury.
Staffordshire: Gnosall, Withmore, Alrewas, Great Madeley, Penkridge, Eccleshall.

But in many cases transforming restoration has largely destroyed any value as historic landmarks, as at Edwalton and Bolsover.

(b) The South Midlands and Welsh Border: Warwickshire, Worcestershire, Monmouthshire, Herefordshire, Shropshire, Cheshire.

Over this wide area of varying geology and material there is no prevailing local type of church, nor, indeed, is this to be expected; all that is practicable here is to indicate a few group varieties in a wide field which would unquestionably repay a close study not yet bestowed on it. There are many standard towers of lime- or sand-stone, attached to quite ordinary average-sized buildings. Fine towers and spires occur occasionally: King's Norton, Solihull, Southam, Ledbury, Weobley, etc., and, as in the North Midlands, the greater town fabrics, such as Ludlow, Coventry, St. Mary's Shrewsbury, possess little local flavour. The churches under the Cotswold ridge, such as Honeybourne and Broadway, really belong to the Cotswold Section of the Limestone Belt (Division 3). Some smaller churches have boarded bellcotes, rudely called "pigeon-house belfries" by nineteenth-century ecclesiologists. *Herefordshire* has several local idiosyncrasies; it shares with Shropshire a severe type of unbuttressed tower, with slightly projecting top, sometimes over a corbel-table (Clungunford, Sutton). There are detached towers, like Bosbury, Richard's Castle, and Garway (connected with the body of the church by a passageway) and those at Pembridge (128) and Yarpole have timber tops in diminishing stages. This design parallels the rather similar Border timber belfry top at Skenfrith, Clun and Rockfield (145), easier to illustrate than to describe. Timber tops of varying kinds are found at Birley, Brimfield and St. Margarets. In the same county are also found dwarf pseudo-transepts (Almeley, Kingsland), and occasionally in fourteenth-century work superlatively long windows reminiscent of Hereford Cathedral north transept, as at Ledbury, Ross, and the two old parish churches of the cathedral city. The occurrence may also be noted of a window on each side above the chancel arch, and a rather unprepossessing local type of three-light Decorated window. The West Country feeling for tall columns is shown in the high octagon piers of Edgmond and Pembridge.

The burly Cheshire towers in red sandstone resemble each other more in feeling than in uniform design, but the county affects a particular variety of battlement which has a well-marked inner line. These occur in profusion on aisles, clerestories, and towers, as at Witton, Northwich, etc., and the local type of Perpendicular tracery is sometimes surmounted by segmental or three-centred arches, even in the clerestories, which differ from the usual Northern square pattern. In fact, the Cheshire folk managed to evolve a quite

146 PIRTON, WORCESTERSHIRE　　147 WARNDON, WORCESTERSHIRE

WEST MIDLAND TIMBERED TOWERS

148 HEYSHAM, LANCASHIRE

149 SKIPWITH, YORKSHIRE

NORTH COUNTRY VILLAGE CHURCHES

able and effective local version in their red sandstone, extending into North Shropshire; the eastern side of the county shows affinities with Lancashire. The fine churches of Astbury, Bunbury, Malpas and Great Budworth will hold their own with the work of any county.

But the most outstanding West Midland feature is the scattered occurrence of timber towers such as Pirton (146) or Warndon (147), or whole fabrics like Melverley, Marton, Old Warburton, Besford and Nether Peover; the two latter interiors are remarkable, Besford especially for its fine roodloft, a feature found at St. Margarets (Herefordshire), though most of the delicate lace-like screens are across the Welsh Border. Little remains of the original timber at Siddington or Stretton Sugwas; indeed, reconstructing restorers, rampant throughout the area, as at Burford, Salop, have been especially heavy-handed on these half-timber fabrics.

7. *The Churches of the North: Northumberland, Durham, Cumberland, Westmorland, Lancashire and Yorkshire.*—With the exception of Yorkshire, it cannot be said that the parish churches of the six northern counties are particularly important or of definite or distinctive type; for many reasons this is by no means surprising, and much of their ancient character has been obliterated by would-be improving restoration. Nevertheless, there is a sort of cousinly likeness generally between many of the fabrics; and it is a truism to say that they express something of the sternness of the landscape in which they are set. Yet such a church as Grinton in Swaledale is not without its austere dignity, and accords well enough with the high fells, the stone cottages and even field buildings surrounding it. There is a resemblance between some of the rather slender towers of the largely Norman and Early English structures of Durham County, and the Lakeland churches show an occasional tower of pele type, with square staircase turret, or throw out a square fortress-like transept. But most churches of the far North are of a rough "small stone" type, occasionally with low-pitched roofs to take the heavy stone slates. The churches of Lancashire have been unjustly abused; many, of couse, have been enlarged or rebuilt, but excellent fabrics remain, constructed of the local sandstone and often having slender spires to their towers; it suffices here to instance Warrington, Halsall, Standish, Aughton and Shepton.

The enormous area of Yorkshire can naturally show every grade of church, of which it is impracticable to attempt the briefest survey here; only a few distinctive characteristics

S

can be indicated. There is an impressive contrast between the two ends of the scale—the spacious magnificence of the large fabrics of growing late-medieval communities, and the austere simplicity of the small moorland buildings. Such fine churches as Thirsk, Rotherham, Howden and Hedon are as splendid as any, but to take two casual instances, Burgwallis and Kirk Sandall are quietly characterful little fellows. The great fabrics of Holderness are not particularly local, and may be regarded in their finished masoncraft as belonging to the Northern end of the limestone belt—Patrington (45), Hemingborough, Holy Trinity, Hull, St. Mary's, Beverley and their sisters. There are fine medium-sized churches scattered around the country, Bedale, Campsall, Ecclesfield, Masham and many another; in Holderness there are places like Preston, but grim little Garton is quite the opposite type.

The average Yorkshire church is long and low, such as Skipwith (149), with flattish roofs for stone slates, and multiple square clerestory windows, often without hood-molds. The square windows may be repeated with rhythmical emphasis all along the aisles, and the porch is generally of one storey and wide-gabled. Sometimes there are plain parapets, or no method of emphasis at all, but often there is a range of battlements along one or both roof lines, punctuated in richer examples by a thin pinnacle to each bay. There is strong resemblance between representative churches from widely distant places in the county, like Skipton, Bedale, Giggleswick, Riccall, Burton Agnes and Sedbergh. But of course there are exceptions and variations—e.g. some buildings plump for arched windows, and some chancels stick to high-pitched roofs.

It is obvious that Yorkshire had a well-developed tower-building tradition, especially in the West Riding. Indeed, the area covered by its work is reckoned the most extensive in all the country. There are towers slim, tall, thick, squat, but generally with four tiny pinnacles; the larger examples are of a well-proportioned and effective massiveness—take, for instance, Fishlake and Almondbury, or Holme-on-Spalding-Moor. The typical tower has twin belfry windows, at Cottingham carried through the storey below; the latter and Tickhill rank with the loveliness of Somerset, and by contrast Halifax achieves a grim stateliness. Many towers are capped with curious forms of open-work parapet, which also surmount some of the attenuated octagonal lanterns found among York parish churches. To the houses of Yorkshire a large work has been devoted; no one has yet essayed a monograph on its churches.

GLOSSARY OF PRINCIPAL TERMS USED

Defined as they apply to the Architecture of the Middle Ages

APSE.—A semicircular or polygonal east end to a church.

ARCADE.—A range of arches supported by columns or piers, either open or "blind," i.e. closed with masonry. Arcading was often used as wall-strengthening decoration. (See *Wall-Arcade*.)

BARREL VAULT.—A covering of either stone or brick, generally of semi-circular section. (Also known as *Wagon Vault*.)

BATTLEMENT.—A parapet cut with indentations at regular intervals, of defensive origin.

BROACH. — The pyramidal masonry filling the four angles where an octagonal spire rises, without parapet, from a square tower.

BUTTRESS.—Masonry built out to strengthen a wall and to resist thrust.

CAPITAL.—The crowning member of a column or pier, giving support to superimposed arches or vaulting ribs.

CHANTRY CHAPEL.—A chapel within or attached to a church, endowed for the saying of Masses for the soul of the testator or others.

CLERESTORY.—The side wall of a church above the aisle roof and nave arcade, usually pierced with windows.

CORBEL.—A block, usually molded or carved, projecting from a wall and supporting a superincumbent weight.

CORBEL-TABLE.—A connected range of corbels immediately beneath the roof of a building; it can also support a parapet.

CRESTING. — Continuous ornament, carved or pierced, surmounting a screen, canopy or cornice.

CROCKETS.—Decorative features occurring principally at the angles of canopies, pinnacles and spires; usually carved and placed equidistantly.

CUSPS.—In tracery, the small inner members that constitute the foliations in the form of trefoils, quatrefoils, etc.

DIAPER ORNAMENT.—An orderly repetition of the same decorative motive, floral, geometrical, etc., carved or painted on a wall surface.

DOG-TOOTH ORNAMENT.—An ornament in the shape of small four-leaf pyramids often set in a hollow molding, and repeated either continuously or at short intervals in thirteenth-century work.

FAN VAULT.—The final development in England of Gothic vaulting, in which the curve of all the ribs is similar. The actual ribs are generally decorative rather than structural, and the fan-like shapes, or *conoids*, are always prominent. Sometimes pendants are introduced.

FINIAL.—A decorative termination to pinnacles, canopies, etc.

FLYING-BUTTRESS.—A buttress in the form of an open arch directing the thrust of a high vault across the roof of an aisle to the main buttress.

GROINED VAULT.—A vault resulting from the intersection of two or more surfaces at an angle, the "arrises," or lines of intersection, being the groins.

HAMMER-BEAM ROOF.—A wooden roof in which the tie-beam is dispensed with, and its place taken by projecting beams. The ends of these are generally treated decoratively.

HOOD-MOLD.—A projecting molding placed for protection around the arch of a window, doorway or arcade. (Also known as *Label-Molding* or *Dripstone*.)

JAMBS.—The upright sides of doorway and window openings.

LABEL-TERMINATION.—A molded or carved termination to a Hood-Mold or Dripstone.

LANCET WINDOW.—A name applied to the narrow pointed window of Early English Gothic from its resemblance to a lancet blade.

LIERNE RIBS.—Small connecting ribs used in vaulting, particularly during the fourteenth century, for decorative effect only.

MISERICORD.—The lifting seat of a chancel stall, usually with a carved bracket on the underside. (Also known as *Miserere*.)

MOLDINGS.—The varieties of contour given to angles, arches and other projecting members of various parts of buildings to produce contrasts of light and shade and richness of effect.

MULLIONS.—The vertical divisions between lights in a Gothic window, from which the tracery springs.

NARTHEX.—A single-storey western vestibule to an early church.

OGEE.—A curve of double flexure, produced by a convex and concave curve flowing the one into the other.

PARAPET.—That part of the external wall of a building, solid, pierced or battlemented, that rises above the level and eaves of a roof.

PARCLOSE.—A screen separating a chapel or aisle from the body of the church.

PIER.—A supporting member from which arches or vaulting spring, in form usually cylindrical, octagonal, rectangular or clustered, i.e. composed of a collection of shafts.

PINNACLE.—A tapering terminating member, vertical, and usually crowned by a finial, and smaller than a turret.

PISCINA.—A recess including a shallow stone basin, with a drain, set in a niche south of an altar for washing sacred vessels.

POUPÉE-HEAD.—The carved termination of a quire-stall or other bench-end. (Sometimes called a *Poppy-head*.)

QUADRIPARTITE.—A simple form of ribbed vaulting, consisting of transverse, diagonal and wall ribs, dividing a rectangular vault space, or compartment, into four segments or "severys."

QUOIN.—The wrought stones at the angles or corners of buildings.

RESPOND.—A half-pillar or corbelled termination to an arcade.

RIB.—A structural member dividing up the compartment of a vault, generally molded.

ROOD-LOFT.—A gallery surmounting the rood-screen, originally supporting the great crucifix or Rood, generally with flanking statues of St. John and the Virgin.

SEDILIA.—Recessed seats for priests on the south side of the high altar, generally of masonry and canopied.

SEXPARTITE.—A form of ribbed vaulting, similar to the quadripartite, but having an extra transverse rib which divides the rectangular compartment into six segments.

SHAFT.—A smaller column, either independent or a member of a pier.

SPANDREL.—The triangular space formed between two arches, or between one arch and the rectangular lines of a hood-mold.

SQUINCH-ARCHES.—Arches thrown across the interior angles of a tower to support an octagonal spire.

STRING-COURSE.—A projecting horizontal band or molding on a wall, often continued around a building.

TABERNACLE-WORK.—The carved and ornamental canopy-work over quire-stalls, fonts, niches, etc.

TRACERY.—The ornamental stonework in the heads of Gothic windows, springing from and supported by the mullions. Circular windows were also filled with tracery. The earliest form is *Plate Tracery*, consisting of circles and other geometrical figures cut in solid stonework. After the middle of the thirteenth century, the tracery was built up of stone bars (*Bar Tracery*).

TRANSOMS.—The horizontal bars in windows.

TRANSEPTS.—The cross-arms of a church, projecting transversely to the nave, chancel and aisles.

TYMPANUM.—The space enclosed between the lintel and the arch of a doorway in Norman and Gothic buildings, often filled with sculpture.

VAULT.—Any form of arched roofing over a building with the exception of the domical. Vaults are either groined, as in Romanesque architecture, or ribbed, as in all Gothic architecture.

WALL-ARCADE.—A blank, or "blind," arcade, used as a form of wall strengthening or decoration, and often richly carved.

INDEX OF ILLUSTRATIONS AND CHIEF
TEXT REFERENCES

ARRANGED UNDER COUNTIES

The references in heavy type are to the *figure numbers* of illustrations.

BEDFORDSHIRE—
Clapham, 67
Dean, 77, 78; **94**
Eaton Bray, 53, 85; **109**
Elstow, 40
Luton, 39
Marston Moretaine, 40, 78
Shillington, 44
Turvey, 85

BERKSHIRE—
Abingdon, 99
Blewbury, 37; **112**
Didcot, 99
Drayton, 81
East Hagbourne, 83
Shottesbrooke, 4, 99
Uffington, 24, 38, 41, 53; **33**
Welford, 99
West Shefford, 99
Windsor, St. George's, 61

BUCKINGHAMSHIRE—
Bletchley, 64
Chesham, 95, 99; **119**
Crawley, 56
Edlesborough, 83
Fingest, **5**
Fulmer, 64
Gayhurst, 65
Ivinghoe, 95
Olney, 99, 102; **83**
Penn, **6**
Stewkley, 32; **28**
Willen, 65
Wing, 24, 31, 44

CAMBRIDGESHIRE—
Bottisham, 80
Cambridge—
All Saints, 40
King's Coll. Chapel, 61
St. Benet's, 47
Cherry Hinton, 55
Elm, 34
Leverington, 103
Long Stanton, 78
March, 77, 79, 108; **91**
Over, 58
Soham, 61

CAMBRIDGESHIRE—*Continued*
Trumpington, 35
Whittlesea, 103

CHESHIRE—
Astbury, 82
Cholmondeley, 64
Nantwich, 58, 73, 80, 83; **103**
Prestbury, 64
Tarvin, 64

CORNWALL—
Altarnun, 82
Blisland, 40
Bodmin, 5, 8, 40, 43; **12**
Breage, 88; **116**
Dulse, 40
Gwennac, 40
Kilkhampton, 107
Launceston, 4, 36, 63, 73, 93, 95, 107; **140**
Lawhitton, 40
Lelant, 106; **120**
Mullion, 106, 107; **13**
Penkivel, 39
Probus, 105
St. Buryan, 106
St. Ives, 106
St. Neots, 69, 93, 106; **142**
St. Stephen-by-Saltash, 40
Telland, 40
Tintagel, 38
Veryan, 40

CUMBERLAND—
Bewcastle, 48

DERBYSHIRE—
Ashbourne, 38
Carrington, 64
Chesterfield, 38, 109
Derby, All Saints', 69
Hope, 103
Mackworth, 42
Melbourne, 32, 35, 40, 50, 68; **56**
Norbury, 58, 87
Repton, 24, 44, 103, 109
Sandiacre, 34
Steetley, 31
Tideswell, 58, 109; **14**

DERBYSHIRE—*Continued*
Wilne, 34
Winster, 79

DEVON—
Alvington, West, **139**
Ashburton, 93, 106; **76**
Atherington, 85
Barnstaple, 105
Bishop's Nympton, 69
Bovey Tracey, **108**
Branscombe, 39
Broadhempston, 4
Chittlehampton, 40, 105
Colyton, 43, 62, 70
Crediton, 38, 105
Cullompton, 36, 74, 78, 85
Dartmouth, 83
Dawlish, 11
Dittisham, 80
East Allington, 83
Exeter, 63, 106
Halberton, 83
Higher Bickington, 82; **92**
Ipplepen, 36, 83, 86, 94; **31**
Kenton, 83
Ottery St. Mary, 40, 74
Plymtree, 85; **106**
Swymbridge, 82
Tiverton, 63, 72, 73; **70**
Totnes, 80
Witheredge, 80
Wolborough, **62, 118**

DORSET—
Blandford, 65; **78**
Melbury Bubb, 40
Puddletown, 22; **138**
Studland, 32
Wareham, 47, 48
Whitechurch Canonicorum, 51

DURHAM—
Brancepeth, 83
Escomb, 23, 47; **50**
Monkwearmouth, 41, 67

ESSEX—
Benfleet, 72
Blackmore, 101; **126**
Castle Hedingham, 51; **57**
Colchester, 47
Copford, 88
Dedham, 40
Feering, 72, 101
Great Baddow, 101
Greenstead, 46; **52**
Laindon, 71
Little Maplestead, 23
Little Tey, 32
Margaretting, 101

ESSEX—*Continued*
Mountnessing, 70
Saffron Walden, 63; **39**
St. Osyth, 101
St. Peter-on-the-Walls, 47
Sandon, 72, 101; **127**
Shenfield, 101
Thaxted, 82; **60**
Thundersley, 101
West Hanningfield, 101
Woodham Walter, 63

GLOUCESTERSHIRE—
Badgeworth, 57
Berkeley, 40, 43
Bisley, 102
Bristol—
    St. Mary Redcliffe, 38, 39, 73
    Temple, 86; **113**
Chipping Campden, 44, 63, 102; **132**
Cirencester, 37, 42, 63, 77, 102; **47**
Cold Ashton, 80
Coln St. Denis, 32, 73
Deerhurst, 39, 47, 48, 67
Duntisbourne Rous, 44
Elkstone, 24, 32, 73; **54**
Fairford, 63, 90; **11**
Gloucester, Cathedral, 60
Harescombe, 70, 97; **123**
Kempley, 88
Mickleton, 102
Northleach, 42, 72, 102
Preston, 70
Thornbury, 70, 102; **133**
Winchcombe, 90, 102
Wyck Rissington, 54

HAMPSHIRE—
Avington, **21**
Basing, 36
Boarhunt, 48
Breamore, 24, 37, 47, 98; **43**
Carisbrooke, I.O.W., 33; *frontispiece*
Crondall, 64, 73
Milford, 40
Nateley Scures, 31, 32
Newport, I.O.W., 83
Odiham, 36, 64
Romsey, 48
St. Mary Bourne, 79
Shorwell, I.O.W., 88
South Hayling, 72
Warblington, 72, 100
Winchfield, 50
Wolverton, 65

HEREFORDSHIRE—
Abbey Dore, 64
Aconbury, 72; **90**
Aymestry, 34
Brampton Brian, 64

HEREFORDSHIRE—*Continued*
Hope Bagot, 70
Kilpeck, 24, 31, 49, 50, 71, 73; **55**
Ledbury, 40, 57, 58
Leominster, 58; **67**
Madley, 44
Pembridge, 40, 58, 110; **128**
Peterchurch, 32
St. Margaret's, 85
Sarnesfield, 68, 98
Tyberton, **80**
Vowchurch, 70
Whitbourne, **8**

HERTFORDSHIRE—
Ayot St. Lawrence, 65
Great Hormead, 85
Hemel Hempstead, 50, 73, 99
Hitchin, 84
Knebworth, 99; **125**
Little Munden, 33
St. Paul's Walden, 85; **81**
Sarratt, 68
Stevenage, 99

HUNTINGDONSHIRE—
Alconbury, 69
Buckden, 78
Bythorn, 103
Fletton, 48
Leighton Bromswold, 64
St. Neots, 78, 102
Spaldwick, 69, 102
Warboys, 69, 102; **134**

KENT—
Barfreston, 50, 55, 71
Boughton Aluph, 101; **131**
Boxley, 42
Brook, 88
Brookland, 40, 71
Canterbury, 47
Charing, 101
Charlton, 64
Chartham, 89, 101
Dover, 38
Dymchurch, 98
Fawkham, 98
Godmersham, 68
Groombridge, 64
Hawkhurst, 58
Hythe, 41
Ingham, 33
Lynsted, 101
Maidstone, 101
Minster, 73
New Romney, 35, 101; **129**
Newington, 101
Otford, 42

KENT—*Continued*
Preston, 68
Reculver, 31
Rochester, 64
Rolvenden, 101
St. Margaret-at-Cliffe, 34, 71
Stone, 53, 54; **58**
Westerham, 101
Westwell, 89
Wrotham, 40

LANCASHIRE—
Furness Abbey, 51
Heysham, **148**
Hornby, 6
Huyton, 79
Warrington, 44

LEICESTERSHIRE—
Ab-Kettleby, 103
Breedon, 48
Gaddesby, 25
Hoby, 58
Kegworth, 58, 109
Kilworth, 54
Kirby Bellairs, 103
Leicester—
  St. Martin's, 17, 78
  St. Mary's, 74
Shepsted, 103
Staunton Harold, 64

LINCOLNSHIRE—
Aunsby, 103
Barton-on-Humber, 23, 47, 48, 67
Billingborough, 58
Boston, 13, 34, 42, 58, 70, 72, 81, 103; **4**
Bottesford, 87, 103
Burgh, 84
Deeping St. James, 51, 59; **73**
Ewerby, 40, 103
Frampton, 39, 55
Frieston, 82
Gedney, 34, 75
Grantham, 40, 43, 56, 69; **66**
Great Ponton, 103
Heckington, 4, 39, 58, 60, 72, 73, 80, 81, 93, 103; **121**
Holbeach, 34, 58, 103
Lincoln, St. Peter's, 67
Long Sutton, 40; **41**
Louth, 69; **9**
Mumby, 54
North Raunceby, 69
Pickworth, 102; **135**
St. Peter-at-Gowts, 67
Stamford, 54, 69
Stow, 47, 49
Swaton, 58, 103

LINCOLNSHIRE—*Continued*
Threckingham, 69, 103
Walcot, 72, 103, 108
Whaplode, 40

MIDDLESEX—
Hayes, 99
Hillingdon, 99
Little Stanmore, 86
London, 5, 43, 44, 55, 64, 65, 66, 79, 83; **77, 84**
Ruislip, 99

MONMOUTHSHIRE—
Caldicote, 42
Newport, St. Woolos, 50; **105**
Rockfield, 110; **145**

NORFOLK—
Acle, 41, 108; **143**
Attleborough, 85, 108
Bessingham, 41; **51**
Billockby, 39
Blakeney, 79
Castle Rising, 71
Cley, 42, 58, 60, 107
Colby, 43
East Dereham, 40, 80, 108; **89**
East Harling, 34, 108; **130**
Filby, 78
Great Yarmouth, 37, 60
Gresham, **13**
Haddiscoe, 68
Hales, 24, 31; **32**
Hardingham, 40
Hingham, 43
Houghton-le-Dale, 55
King's Lynn—
St. Margaret's, 40, 83
St. Nicholas', 30, 42, 62, 72, 82; **88**
Knapton, 77, 79, 108
Little Ellingham, 40
Ludham, 17
Necton, 77, 79; **93**
North Walsham, 82
Norwich, St. Peter Mancroft, 63, 107; **75**
Pulham Magdalen, 77
Pulham St. Mary, 72, 108
Ranworth, 85
Redenhall, 108
Sall, 42, 69, 83
Snettisham, 58
South Burlingham, 83; **104**
Starston, 78
Terrington St. Clement, 63, 82; **37**
Thornage, 39
Thorpe, 68
Tilney All Saints, 32, 34, 108; **34**

NORFOLK—*Continued*
Trunch, 43, 72, 79, 82, 108
Walpole St. Peter, 34, 41, 63, 82, 108; **17, 29**
Walsoken, 32, 35, 50, 51
West Walton, 40, 53, 55; **46, 59, 64**
Wiggenhall, 82; **102**
Worstead, 43
Wymondham, 80

NORTHAMPTONSHIRE—
Aldwinckle, 89, 102, 103
Barnack, 47, 48, 67, 71
Barnwell St. Andrew, 69
Brixworth, 24, 39, 41, 44, 47, 48; **25**
Castor, 38, 68
Crick, 56, 58, 72
Croughton, 88
Earl's Barton, 47, 48, 67; **82**
Etton, 68, 103
Finedon, 58, 59, 103
Fotheringay, 4, 8, 59, 70, 103
Great Brington, 53; **61**
Harleston, 56
Higham Ferrers, 43, 54, 56, 58, 59, 72, 78, 84, 87, 103; **86**
Islip, 43
Kettering, 69, 102
King's Sutton, 42, 102
Little Addington, 72
Lowick, 70, 103; **111**
Luddington, 69
Northampton, 23, 50; **53**
Northborough, 55
Oundle, 43, 55, 102; **7**
Passenham, 64
Polebrook, 51
Raunds, 36, 43, 54, 69, 102
Ringstead, 58
Rushden, 39, 43
Stanford-on-Avon, 89
Stanwick, 41
Stowe-Nine-Churches, 64
Tilbrook, 102
Titchmarsh, 102
Wadenhoe, 68
Wakerley, 50
Wansford, 47
Warmington, 51, 53, 54, 72
Whiston, 59, 62, 63, 102, 103
Wilby, 41, 103, 108
Woodford, 56, 59, 103; **137**
Yelverton, 62

NOTTINGHAMSHIRE
Hawton, 43, 58, 80, 81; **95**
Holme, 103
Keyworth, 40
Newark, 39, 44, 60, 83
Nottingham, 87

OXFORDSHIRE—
Adderbury, 4, 8, 75, 78, 80, 102
Bampton, 38, 72, 81, 102; **97**
Broughton, 35
Burford, 37, 43, 102
Chipping Norton, 34, 43, 102
Clanfield, 98
Ewelme, 36, 77, 82, 87
Great Tew, 102
Hampton Poyle, 56
Iffley, 50, 71
Langford, 48
Long Coombe, 80, 89
North Leigh, 74
Oxford—
St. Giles', 56
St. Peter's in the East, 44
St. Mary's, 80
Rycote, 82
Somerton, 81
Standlake, 41
Stanton Harcourt, 89
Witney, 38, 42, 44, 53, 102; **24**
Woodstock, 42, 56
Yelford, 98

RUTLAND—
Ayston, 35
Etton, 53
Exton, 103
Ketton, 102, 103; **85**
Little Casterton, 103
Lyddington, 102
Manton, 70, 98, 103
Upper Hambleton, 102; **136**

SHROPSHIRE—
Acton Burnell, 4, 38
Battlefield, 4
Diddlebury, 48
Heath Chapel, 50; **27**
Hopton Cangeford, 65
Ludlow, 23, 62, 63, 72, 83, 90, 110; **98**
Shrewsbury, 38, 52, 65
Stanton Lacy, 47

SOMERSET—
Axbridge, 105
Bishop's Lydeard, 82, 104
Broomfield, 82
Bruton, 43, 63, 72, 105
Brympton, 70
Burrington, 73
Cheddar, 104
Compton Bishop, 34
Compton Martin, 33
Croscombe, 18, 64, 83, 85; **20**
Crowcombe, **87**
Culbone, **15, 16**
T

SOMERSET—*Continued*
Curry, Rivel, **71**
Doulting, 41, 70, 105; **44**
Dundry, 70, 105
Elm, 68
Evercreech, 105
Farleigh Hungerford, 86
Huish Episcopi, 104; **141**
Ilminster, 69
Leigh-on-Mendip, 69, 105
Martock, 77
North Petherton, 105
Shepton Mallet, 105
Taunton, 69, 105
Wedmore, 86; **22**
Wellow, 81, 105
Wells, 25, 52, 77, 81, 105; **38, 49**
Weston-in-Gordano, 42
Winscomb, 89
Wrington, 73, 105; **3**

STAFFORDSHIRE—
Blore Ray, 84
Elford, 87

SUFFOLK—
Bamford, 80
Blythborough, 83
Boxford, 72
Bury St. Edmunds, St. Mary's, 34, 107; **40**
Coddenham, 107
Copdock, 62
Dennington, 83, 84; **107**
Eye, 42, 72, 94, 107, 108; **144**
Framlingham, 83, 87; **110**
Fressingfield, 82, 83
Herringfleet, 68
Kedington, 82
Lavenham, 4, 6, 34, 36, 62, 77, 94, 107, 108; **35, 72, 96**
Long Melford, 34, 107; **10, 74, 99**
Lowestoft, 62
Rickinghall Inferior, 56
Somerleyton, 85; **117**
Ufford, 82, 108; **100**
Walsham le Willows, 77
Wenhaston, 89
Winford, 104
Wingfield, 6, 10, 83, 87
Winston, 72
Woolpit, 42, 79, 82
Worlingworth, 82

SURREY—
Chaldon, 34, 89
Chipstead, 98
Compton, 73
Crowhurst, 98, 100
Elstead, 98
Great Bookham, 70, 100; **48**

SURREY—*Continued*
Guildford, 73
Merstham, 34, 68, 100; **124**
Ockham, 53
Oxted, 100
Shere, 34, 100
Thursley, 71, 100

SUSSEX—
Arundel, 80
Bishopstone, 41, 67
Bosham, 53
Bury, 100
Clymping, 40, 68, 100
Coates, 70
Cocking, 100
Coombes, 100
Dallington, 100
Etchingham, 23
Ford, 70
Glynde, **79**
Heathfield, 100
Heyshott, 98, 100
Horsham, 34
Litlington, 71, 94, 98; **122**
Newhaven, 31, 68, 100
Old Shoreham, 24, 38, 68; **42**
Sompting, 47
South Harting, 79
Steyning, 100
Tangmere, 98
West Chiltington, 88
Wilmington, 100
Worth, 24, 31
Yapton, 42, 100

WARWICKSHIRE—
Brownsover, 54
Coleshill, 79
Compton Wynyates, 64
Coventry, 5, 37, 69, 110
Halford, 34
Ilmington, 34
Long Compton, 102
Stratford-on-Avon, **36**
Temple Balsall, 56
Warmington, 44
Warwick, 40, 87
Wroxall, 42

WESTMORLAND—
Kirkby Stephen, 39

WILTSHIRE—
Amesbury, 38, 95
Avebury, 104
Biddestone, 23
Bradford-on-Avon, 24, 41, 47; **26**
Christian Malford, 84
Cricklade, 95
Devizes, St. John's, 38, 68, 73; **30**
Edington, 61; **69**
Malmesbury, 43
Potterne, 53, 95
Salisbury, St. Thomas, 89; **19, 115**
Steeple Ashton, 104
Wanborough, 104
Winterbourne Dauntsey, 88

WORCESTERSHIRE—
Bredon, 32, 51
Chaddesley Corbet, 79
Crowle, 80
Elmley Castle, **114**
Evesham, 62, 80
Hanley, 63
Norton, 80
Pirton, 111; **146**
Warndon, 111; **147**

YORKSHIRE—
Adel, 32, 50, 71
Almondbury, 89
Beverley, St. Mary's, 6, 62, 112; **68**
Coxwold, 41
Filey, 34
Fountains Abbey, 51
Halifax, 82; **101**
Hedon, 58
Howden, 58
Kirksandal, 84
Kirkstall Abbey, 51
Leeds, St. John's, 18, 63
Patrington, 38, 39, 58, 62, 69, 81; **45, 63, 65**
Pickering, 88
Roos, 43
Rossington, 83
Skelton, 53, 54, 71
Skipwith, 85, 94, 112; **149**
Stillingfleet, 85
Tickhill, 62, 69, 112
Watton, 63
Wawn, 55
Whitby, 83; **23**
York, 90

INDEX TO TEXT AND ILLUSTRATIONS

The references in heavy type are to the *figure numbers* of illustrations.

To keep the Index within manageable compass, it has not been found practicable, or considered advisable, to include a reference to every one of the large number of churches incidentally mentioned.

Abbey Dore, 64
Abingdon, St. Helen's, 99
Ab-Kettleby, 103
Acle, 41, 108; **143**
Aconbury, 72; **90**
Acton Burnell, 4, 38
Adderbury, 4, 8, 75, 78, 80, 102
Adel, 32, 50, 71
Alabaster, works in, 81, 87; **2, 99, 111**
Alconbury, 69
Aldwinckle, 89, 102, 103
Almondbury, 89
Altarnun, 82
Alvington, West, **139**
Amesbury, 38, 95
Arcades, 32, 51, 54, 59
Arches, 49, 51, 54, 57, 62
Arundel, 80
Ashbourne, 38
Ashburton, 93, 106; **76**
Astbury, 82
Aston Eyre, 49
Atherington, 85
Attleborough, 85, 108
Aunsby, 103
Avebury, 104
Avington, **21**
Axbridge, 105
Aymestry, 34
Ayot St. Lawrence, 65
Ayston, 35

Badgeworth, 57
Ballflower ornament, 57; **67**
Bamford, 80
Bampton, 38, 72, 81, 102; **97**
Barfreston, 50, 55, 71
Barnack, 47, 48, 67, 71
Barnstaple, 105
Barnwell St. Andrew, 69
Barton-on-Humber, 23, 47, 48, 67
Basing, 36
Battlefield, 4
Bedfordshire churches, 99
Belfries, 40, 70, 98; **128, 145**
Benfleet, 72
Berkeley, 40, 43
Berkshire churches, 99
Bessingham, 41; **51**
Beverley, St. Mary's, 6, 62, 112; **68**

Bewcastle, 48
Biddestone, 23
Billingborough, 58
Billockby, 39
Bishop's Lydeard, 82, 104
Bishop's Nympton, 69
Bishopstone, 41, 67
Bisley, 102
Blackmore, 101; **126**
Blakeney, 79
Blandford, 65; **78**
Bletchley, 64
Blewbury, 37; **112**
Blisland, 40
Blore Ray, 84
Blythburgh, 83
Boarhunt, 48
Bodmin, 5, 8, 40, 43; **12**
Bosham, 53
Boston, 34, 42, 58, 70, 72, 81, 103; **4**
Bottesford, 87, 103
Bottisham, 80
Boughton Aluph, 101; **131**
Bovey Tracey, **108**
Boxford, 72
Boxley, 42
Bradford-on-Avon, 24, 41, 47; **26**
Brampton Brian, 64
Brancepeth, 83
Branscombe, 39
Breage, 88; **116**
Breamore, 24, 37, 47, 98; **43**
Bredon, 32, 51
Breedon, 48
Bristol—
 St. Mary Redcliffe, 38, 39, 73
 Temple, 86; **113**
Brixworth, 24, 39, 41, 44, 47, 48; **25**
Broadhempston, 4
Brook, 88
Brookland, 40, 71
Broomfield, 82
Broughton, 35
Brownsover, 54
Bruton, 43, 63, 72, 105
Brympton, 70
Buckden, 78
Buckinghamshire churches, 99
Burford, 37, 43, 102
Burgh, 84

Burrington, 73
Bury, 100
Bury St. Edmunds, 34, 107; **40**
Buttresses, 54
Bythorn, 102

Caldicote, 42
Cambridge—
  All Saints', 40
  King's Coll. Chapel, 61
  St. Benet's, 46
Canterbury, 47
Capitals, 50, 53, 62; **62, 63, 64**
Carisbrooke, 33; *frontispiece*
Carrington, 64
Carving, stone, 48, 73, 79; **13, 55, 95, 97, 113**
Castle Hedingham, 51; **57**
Castle Rising, 71
Castor, 38, 68
Chaddesley Corbet, 79
Chaldon, 34, 89
Chantry chapels, 6, 36 ff.
Charing, 101
Charlton, 64
Chartham, 89, 101
Cheddar, 104
Cherry Hinton, 55
Chesham, 95, 99; **119**
Chesterfield, 38, 109
Chipping Campden, 44, 63, 102; **132**
Chipping Norton, 34, 43, 102
Chipstead, 98
Chittlehampton, 40, 105
Cholmondeley, 64
Christian Malford, 84
Cirencester, 37, 42, 63, 77, 102; **47**
Cistercian buildings, 51
Clanfield, 98
Clapham, 67
Clerestories, 33 ff., 101, 105
Cley, 42, 58, 60, 107
Clymping, 40, 68, 100
Coates, 70
Cocking, 100
Coddenham, 107
Colby, 43
Colchester, 47
Cold Ashton, 80
Coleshill, 79
Coln St. Denis, 32, 73
Colyton, 43, 62, 70
Compton, 73
Compton Bishop, 34
Compton Martin, 33
Compton Wynyates, 64
Contracts, building, 8
Coombes, 100
Copdock, 62
Copford, 88
Cornish Churches, 106
Coventry, 5, 37, 69, 110

Coxwold, 41
Crawley, 56
Crediton, 38, 105
Crick, 56, 58, 72
Cricklade, 95
Crondall, 64, 73
Croscombe, 18, 64, 83, 85; **20**
Croughton, 88
Crowcombe, **87**
Crowhurst, 98, 100
Crowle, 80
Crypts, 44
Culbone, **15, 16**
Cullompton, 36, 74, 78, 85
Curry Rivel, **71**

Dallington, 100
Dartmouth, 83
Dawlish, 11
Dean, 77, 78; **94**
Dedham, 40
Deeping St. James, 51, 59; **73**
Deerhurst, 39, 47, 48, 67
De Leighton, Thomas, smith, 85
Dennington, 83, 84; **107**
Derby, All Saints, 69
Devizes, St. John's, 38, 68, 73; **30**
Devon churches, 105
Didcot, 99
Diddlebury, 48
Dittisham, 80
Dog-tooth ornament, 53, 54
Doorways, 49, 62, 71
Dorset churches, 104
Doulting, 41, 70, 105; **44**
Dover, 38
Drayton, 81
Dulse, 40
Dundry, 70, 105
Duntisbourne Rous, 44
Dymchurch, 98

Earl's Barton, 47, 48, 67; **82**
Easby, paintings, 88
East Allingham, 83
East Anglian churches, 107
East Dereham, 40, 80, 108; **89**
East Hagbourne, 83
East Harling, 34, 108; **130**
Eaton Bray, 53, 85; **109**
Edington, 61; **69**
Edlesborough, 83
Elford, 87
Elkstone, 24, 32, 73; **54**
Elm (Cambs), 34
Elm (Somerset), 68
Elmley Castle, **114**
Elstead, 98
Elstow, 40
Escomb, 23, 47; **50**
Essex churches, 100

Etchingham, 23
Etton (Northants), 68, 103
Etton (Rutland), 53
Evercreech, 105
Evesham, 62, 80
Ewelme, 36, 77, 82, 87
Ewerby, 40, 103
Exeter, St. Petrock's, 63, 106
Exton, 103
Eye, 42, 72, 94, 107, 108; **144**

Fairford, 63, 90; **11**
Farleigh Hungerford, 86
Fawkham, 98
Feering, 72, 101
Filby, 78
Finedon, 58, 59, 103
Fingest, **5**
Fletton, 48
Flintwork, 41, 42, 72, 99, 107
Fonts, 58, 79, 82, 86; **13, 89, 100, 101**
Ford, 70
Fotheringay, 4, 8, 59, 70, 103
Fountains Abbey, 51
Framlingham, 83, 87; **110**
Frampton, 39, 55
Fressingfield, 82, 83
Frieston, 82
Fulmer, 64
Furness Abbey, 51

Gables, 34; **129**
Gaddesby, 25
Gayhurst, 65
Gedney, 34, 75
Gilds, 5 ff., 26 ff.
Glass, 89
Gloucester, Cathedral, 60
Gloucestershire churches, 102
Glynde, **79**
Godmersham, 68
Grantham, 40, 43, 56, 69; **66**
Great Baddow, 101
Great Bookham, 70, 100; **48**
Great Brington, 53; **61**
Great Hormead, 85
Great Ponton, 103
Great Tew, 102
Great Yarmouth, 37, 60
Greenstead, 46; **52**
Gresham, **13**
Groombridge, 64
Guildford, 73
Gwennac, 40

Haddiscoe, 68
Halberton, 83
Hales, 24, 31; **32**
Halford, 34
Halifax, 82; **101**
Hammerbeam roofs, 64, 77; **91, 93**
Hampshire churches, 100

Hampton Poyle, 56
Hanley, 63
Hardingham, 40
Harescombe, 70, 97; **123**
Harleston, 56
Hawkhurst, 58
Hawton, 43, 58, 80, 81; **95**
Hayes, 99
Heath Chapel, 50; **27**
Heathfield, 100
Heckington, 4, 39, 58, 60, 72, 73, 80,
     81, 93, 103; **121**
Hedon, 58
Hemel Hempstead, 50, 73, 99
Herringfleet, 68
Hertfordshire churches, 99
Heysham, **148**
Heyshott, 98, 100
Higham Ferrers, 43, 54, 56, 58, 59, 72,
     78, 84, 87, 103; **86**
Higher Bickington, 82; **92**
Hillingdon, 99
Hingham, 43
Hitchin, 84
Holbeach, 34, 58, 103
Holme, 103
Hope, 103
Hope Bagot, 70
Hopton Cangeford, 65
Hornby, 6
Horsham, 34
Horwood, William, mason, 8
Houghton-le-Dale, 55
Howden, 58
Huish Episcopi, 104; **141**
Huyton, 79
Hythe, 41

Iffley, 50, 71
Ilmington, 34
Ilminster, 69
Ingham, 33
Ipplepen, 36, 83, 86, 94; **31**
Ironwork, 85; **109**
Islip, 43
Ivinghoe, 95

Kedington, 82
Kegworth, 58, 109
Kempley, 88
Kent churches, 101
Kenton, 83
Kettering, 69, 102
Ketton, 102, 103; **85**
Keyworth, 40
Kilkhampton, 107
Kilpeck, 24, 31, 49, 50, 71, 73; **55**
Kilworth, 54
King's Lynn—
     St. Margaret's, 40, 83
     St. Nicholas, 30, 42, 62, 72, 82; **88**

King's Sutton, 42, 102
Kirby Bellairs, 103
Kirkby Stephen, 39
Kirksandal, 84
Kirkstall Abbey, 51
Knapton, 77, 79, 108
Knebworth, 99; **125**

Laindon, 71
Langford, 48
Launceston, 4, 36, 63, 73, 93, 95, 107; **140**
Lavenham, 4, 6, 34, 36, 62, 77, 94, 107, 108; **35, 72, 96**
Lawhitton, 40
Ledbury, 40, 57, 58
Leeds, St. John's, 18, 63
Leicester—
    St. Martin's, 17, 18
    St. Mary's, 74
Leigh-on-Mendip, 69, 105
Leighton Bromswold, 64
Lelant, 106; **120**
Leominster, 58; **67**
Leverington, 103
Lincoln, St. Peter's, 67
Litlington, 71, 94, 98; **122**
Little Addington, 72
Little Casterton, 103
Little Ellingham, 40
Little Maplestead, 23
Little Munden, 33
Little Stanmore, 86
Little Tey, 32
London, City Churches, 5, 43, 44, 55, 64, 65, 66, 79, 83; **77, 84**
Long Compton, 102
Long Coombe, 80, 89
Long Melford, 34, 107; **10, 74, 99**
Long Stanton, 78
Long Sutton, 40; **41**
Louth, 69; **9**
Lowestoft, 62
Lowick, 70, 103; **111**
Luddington, 69
Ludham, 17
Ludlow, 23, 62, 63, 72, 83, 90, 110; **98**
Luton, 39
Lych gates, **145**
Lyddington, 102
Lynsted, 101

Mackworth, 42
Madley, 44
Maidstone, 101
Malmesbury, 43
Manton, 70, 98, 103
March, 77, 79, 108; **91**
Margaretting, 101
Marston Moretaine, 40, 78

Martock, 77
Materials, building, 46 ff., 49, 60, 95 ff.
Melbourne, 32, 35, 40, 50, 68; **56**
Melbury Bubb, 40
Merstham, 34, 68, 100; **124**
Mickleton, 102
Middlesex churches, 99
Midland churches, 103, 109 ff.
Milford, 40
Minster, 73
Moldings, 49, 53, 60, 62
Monkwearmouth, 41, 67
Monuments, 86; **110, 111, 113, 114**
Mountnessing, 70
Mullion, 106, 107; **18**
Mumby, 54

Nantwich, 58, 73, 80, 83; **103**
Nateley Scures, 31, 32
Naves, 15, 16, 73 ff.; **59, 60**
Necton, 77, 79; **93**
New Romney, 36, 101; **129**
Newark, 39, 44, 60, 83
Newhaven, 31, 68, 100
Newington, 101
Newport, I.O.W., 83
Newport, St. Woolos, 50; **105**
Norbury, 58, 87
North, churches of the, 111
North Leigh, 74
North Petherton, 105
North Raunceby, 69
North Walsham, 82
Northampton, 23, 50; **53**
Northamptonshire churches, 102
Northborough, 55
Northleach, 42, 72, 102
Norton, 80
Norwich, St. Peter Mancroft, 63, 107; **75**
Nottingham, 87

Ockham, 53
Odiham, 36, 64
Old Shoreham, 24, 38, 68; **42**
Olney, 99, 102; **83**
Ornament, 49, 53 ff., 57, 58, 63, 72
Otford, 42
Ottery St. Mary, 40, 74
Oundle, 43, 55, 102; **7**
Over, 58
Oxford—
    St. Giles', 56
    St. Mary's, 80
    St. Peter's in the East, 44
Oxted, 100

Painting, 88; **115, 116, 117, 118**
Passenham, 64
Patrington, 38, 39, 58, 62, 69, 81; **45, 63, 65**
Pembridge, 40, 110, 158; **128**

Penkivel, 39
Penn, **6**
Peterchurch, 32
Pickering, 88
Pickworth, 102; **135**
Piers, 58, 62, 108
Pirton, 111; **146**
Piscinas, 42, 43
Plans, church, 23 ff., 35 ff.
Plymtree, 85; **106**
Polebrook, 51
Porches, 39, 41 ff., 71 ff; **47, 87, 88, 90**
Potterne, 53, 95
Prestbury, 64
Preston (Glos.), 70
Preston (Kent), 68
Probus, 105
Puddletown, 22; **138**
Pulham Magdalen, 77
Pulham St. Mary, 72, 108
Pulpits, 64, 80, 83; **23**

Ranworth, 85
Raunds, 36, 43, 54, 69, 72, 102
Reculver, 31
Redenhall, 108
Renaissance, 63 ff., 85, 86; **20, 21, 78, 79, 80, 81, 84, 114**
Repton, 24, 44, 103, 109
Reredoses, 81
Rickinghall Inferior, 56
Ringstead, 58
Rochester, 64
Rockfield, 110; **145**
Rolvenden, 101
Romsey, 48
Rood Screens, 36; **106, 107**
Roofs, 74 ff., 105; **91, 93, 94, 140**
Roos, 43
Rossington, 83
Ruislip, 99
Rushden, 39, 43
Rycote, 82

Saffron Walden, 63; **39**
St. Buryan, 106
St. Ives, 106
St. Margaret-at-Cliffe, 34, 71
St. Margaret's, 85
St. Mary Bourne, 79
St. Neot's (Cornwall), 69, 93, 106; **142**
St. Neots (Hunts), 78, 102
St. Osyth, 101
St. Paul's Walden, 85; **81**
St. Peter-at-Gowts, 67
St. Peter-on-the-Walls, 47
St. Stephen-by-Saltash, 40
Salisbury, 89; **19, 115**
Sall, 42, 69, 83
Sandiacre, 34

Sandon, 72, 101; **127**
Sarnesfield, 68, 98
Sarratt, 68
Screens, 84, 104; **104, 106, 107, 108, 117, 118**
Sculpture, 53 ff.; **95, 97, 99, 110, 111, 113, 114**
Sedilia, 58, 80
Shenfield, 101
Shepsted, 103
Shepton Mallet, 105
Shere, 34, 100
Shillington, 44
Shorwell, 88
Shottesbrooke, 4, 99
Shrewsbury, 38, 52, 65
Skelton, 53, 54, 71
Skipwith, 85, 94, 112; **149**
Snettisham, 58
Soham, 61
Somerleyton, 85; **117**
Somerset churches, 104
Somerton, 81
Sompting, 47
South Burlingham, 83; **104**
South Harting, 79
South Hayling, 72
Southwold, 72, 77, 83, 107
Spaldwick, 69, 102
Spires, 67 ff., 102 ff.; **119, 134, 135, 136**
Stamford, 54, 69
Standlake, 41
Stanford-on-Avon, 89
Stanton Harcourt, 89
Stanton Lacy, 47
Stanwick, 41
Starston, 78
Staunton Harold, 64
Steeple Ashton, 104
Steeples, 71; **119**
Steetley, 31
Stevenage, 99
Stewkley, 32; **28**
Steyning, 100
Stillingfleet, 85
Stone, 53, 54; **58**
Stow, 47, 49
Stowe-Nine-Churches, 64
Stratford-on-Avon, **36**
Studland, 32
Styles, architectural, 45 ff.
Sussex churches, 100
Swaton, 58, 103
Swymbridge, 82

Tangmere, 98
Tarvin, 64
Taunton, 69, 105
Telland, 40
Temple Balsall, 56

Terrington St. Clement, 63, 82; **37**
Thaxted, 82; **60**
Thornage, 39
Thornbury, 70, 102; **133**
Thorpe, 68
Threckingham, 69, 103
Thundersley, 101
Thursley, 71, 100
Tickhill, 62, 69, 112
Tideswell, 58, 109; **14**
Tilbrook, 102
Tilney, All Saints, 32, 34, 108; **34**
Tintagel, 38
Titchmarsh, 102
Tiverton, 63, 72, 73; **70**
Totnes, 80
Towers, 39 ff., 67 ff., 102 ff.; **133, 141, 142, 143, 144, 146, 147**
Tracery, 54, 56, 57, 58, 62; **66, 67, 68, 69**
Trumpington, 35
Trunch, 43, 72, 79, 82, 108
Turvey, 85
Tyberton, **80**

Uffington, 24, 38, 41, 53; **33**
Ufford, 82, 108; **100**
Upper Hambleton, 102; **13**

Vaulting, 73; **54**
Veryan, 40
Vestry, 43
Vowchurch, 70

Wadenhoe, 68
Wakerley, 50
Walcot, 72, 103, 108
Walpole St. Peter, 34, 41, 63, 82, 108; **17, 29**
Walsham le Willows, 77
Walsoken, 32, 35, 50, 51
Wanborough, 104
Wansford, 47
Warblington, 72, 100
Warboys, 69, 102; **134**
Wareham, 47, 48
Warmington, 44, 51, 53, 54, 72
Warndon, 111; **147**
Warrington, 44
Warwick, 40, 87
Watton, 63
Wawn, 55
Wedmore, 86; **22**
Welford, 99
Wellow, 81, 105
Wells, 25, 52, 77, 81, 105; **38, 49**
Wenhaston, 89

West Chiltington, 88
West Hanningfield, 101
West Shefford, 99
West Walton, 40, 53, 55; **46, 59, 64**
Westerham, 101
Weston-in-Gordano, 42
Westwell, 89
Whaplode, 40
Whiston, 62, 63, 102, 103
Whitbourne, **8**
Whitby, 83; **23**
Whitechurch Canonicorum, 51
Whittlesea, 103
Wiggenhall, 82; **102**
Wilby, 41, 103, 108
Willen, 65
Wilmington, 100
Wilne, 34
Wiltshire churches, 104
Winchcombe, 90, 102
Winchcombe (Mason), 8
Winchfield, 50
Windows, style in, 53 ff., 62; **24, 40, 45, 61, 67, 68, 69**
Windsor, St. George's, 61
Winford, 104
Wing, 24, 31, 44
Wingfield, 6, 10, 83, 87
Winscomb, 89
Winster, 79
Winston, 72
Winterbourne Dauntsey, 88
Witheredge, 80
Witney, 38, 42, 44, 53, 102; **24**
Wolborough, **62, 118**
Wolverton, 65
Woodford, 56, 59, 103; **137**
Woodham Walter, 63
Woodstock, 42, 56
Woodwork, examples of, 77, 81 ff.; **14, 92, 98, 100, 101, 102, 103, 104, 106, 108**
Woolpit, 42, 79, 82
Worlingworth, 82
Worstead, 43
Worth, 24, 31
Wrexham, 70
Wrington, 73, 105; **3**
Wrotham, 40
Wroxall, 42
Wyck Rissington, 54
Wymondham, 80
Wynchecombe, Geoffrey, 5

Yapton, 42, 100
Yelford, 98
Yelverton, 62
York, 90